THE ARMY OF
ALEXANDER
THE GREAT

THE ARMY OF
ALEXANDER THE GREAT

STEPHEN ENGLISH

Pen & Sword
MILITARY

First published in Great Britain in 2009 by
Pen & Sword Military
An imprint of
Pen & Sword Books Ltd
47 Church Street
Barnsley
South Yorkshire
S70 2AS

ISBN 978 1 84415 839 3

A CIP catalogue record for this book is
available from the British Library

Typeset in 11.5pt Ehrhardt
by S L Menzies-Earl

Printed and bound in England
by CPI UK

Pen & Sword Books Ltd incorporates the imprints of
Pen & Sword Aviation, Pen & Sword Maritime, Pen & Sword Military, Wharncliffe
Local History, Pen & Sword Select,
Pen & Sword Military Classics and Leo Cooper.

For a complete list of Pen & Sword titles please contact
PEN & SWORD BOOKS LIMITED
47 Church Street, Barnsley, South Yorkshire, S70 2AS, England
E-mail: enquiries@pen-and-sword.co.uk
Website: www.pen-and-sword.co.uk

Contents

—⚂—

List of Illustrations

—⚄—

Acknowledgements

—⚉—

This book arose out of a master's degree thesis that I completed in 2002; it was never intended for publication, merely as a learning experience, and a stepping stone to a doctorate. Having said that, I have enjoyed the process of turning it into a book and there are a number of people I would like to thank for making the present work happen. There are many people that deserve credit, and my eternal thanks for helping in the production of this book. Firstly, Hans Van Wees for agreeing to be the external moderator on the original thesis and on the subsequent doctorate, and for his helpful comments and encouragement towards my continued studies. My editor, Philip Sidnell, is deserving of great praise for his many useful comments on the various drafts of this book, as well as his help in finding and selecting the plates and answering my endless questions with great patience and skill. Thanks too to Pen & Sword Books for making the foolish decision to take a chance on a new author; I hope to have rewarded their faith. With regards to editors and publishers, I would also like to thank Jasper Oorthuys of *Ancient Warfare Magazine* for agreeing to publish my first attempt at writing in his excellent magazine, and helping with the illustrations for this book.

I would also like to thank Elizabeth, for being wonderful, for putting up with me, and for her constant support and encouragement in our life together. My thanks also to my parents for their encouragement over the long years; and my brother, John, for his tireless (and, I'm happy to say, free) IT support. I must also mention Martin and Sue Foulkes; Sue for her boundless enthusiasm and encouragement and Martin for his help and guidance as a study partner during our seven years together in Durham University.

My greatest thanks are reserved, however, for Professor Peter Rhodes: for over a decade since 1997 Peter has been my lecturer, tutor, supervisor, mentor and for my part at least, friend. His kindness and patience and academic expertise have been limitless and invaluable to me over that time, truly I would not have achieved anywhere near the level of academic success that I have without him. He will always remain the standard to which I aspire, but will never reach. Peter, 'thank you' simply does not seem enough.

Foreword

—⚏—

Stephen English came to the University of Durham in 1997 to study ancient history, and since 2000 has been working on Alexander the Great. As a preliminary to a full study of Alexander's campaigns he began with a re-examination of Alexander's army, and the fruits of that re-examination are presented here. After a series of chapters devoted to the different components of Alexander's forces, he concludes with the command structure, and a chapter which illustrates Alexander's use of his forces by focusing on three campaigns of different kinds: the fighting in the Balkans in 335, before Alexander crossed to Asia; the battle of Issus in 333, when Alexander encountered the Persian king, Darius, for the first time; and the siege of Tyre in 332, in which Alexander built on recent developments in siege machinery to capture a strongly fortified island city. Stephen English is well read in the ancient sources and modern studies, and is the first author for a long time to grapple with the full range of problems in order to provide a comprehensive account of Alexander's forces. This will be an essential book for all who are interested in Alexander the Great.

P. J. Rhodes
Honorary Professor of Ancient History, University of Durham

Introduction

—∿—

With a small army, but distinguished for its intrinsic perfection,
Alexander overthrew the decayed fabric of the Asiatic States:
Without rest, and regardless of risks, he traversed the breadth of Asia[1]

Probably in 359* Philip of Macedon inherited a shambles of a kingdom; beset on all sides by enemies and with its army having suffered a massive recent defeat. Within the space of thirty-five years the Macedonian state rose to rule the majority of the known world, having conquered the largest and most powerful empire the world had yet seen: Persia. This book is intended to be an examination of the tools with which that remarkable turn around was achieved: the army. Philip and Alexander forged an army that was unparalleled in the ancient world, an army that was capable of campaigning at any time of year and in any terrain that Greece or Persia had to offer. They showed themselves capable of adapting to any new conditions and of overcoming any obstacle placed in their path, be it natural or man made. Once they crossed the Hellespont, most of the army did not see Greece again for eleven years; the fact that the army showed very few signs of dissatisfaction or rebellion until the Opis mutiny demonstrates their own discipline and belief in the campaign, as well as Alexander's incredible personal charisma and leadership ability.

The purpose of this book is not to be an examination of Alexander's campaigns, although examples are used to illustrate individual points, but to be an examination specifically of the army. In the interests of completeness, however, the final chapter is devoted to an examination of three of Alexander's most significant campaigns, those of Greece, Issus and Tyre; these three campaigns allow us to examine Alexander's generalship as well as his tactics and strategies. More importantly than this, they allow us to see the army in action in a range of different terrains and situations, from the mountains of Northern Greece, to the Plain of Issus and the seminal siege of Tyre. These three campaigns clearly demonstrate the versatility of the army, its discipline and its tactics.

* All dates are BC unless otherwise stated.

The career of Alexander the Great is essentially one long and almost unbroken campaign lasting some eleven years. With this in mind it is somewhat surprising that his army has received relatively little attention from modern scholars: even his campaigns are underrepresented in the literature, with most preferring to write thinly-veiled biographies of Alexander himself. This book intends, in some small way, to redress the balance in favour of the study of military history; sadly no longer fashionable.

Historians of any period are faced with the difficulties of historiography, but these difficulties are particularly acute for the ancient historian given the temporal gap between us and our subject. This difficulty is magnified yet further with any study of Alexander, as the first surviving source was written some four centuries after his death. We can only imagine the mysteries that could be solved by access to the lost histories of Ptolemy or Callisthenes; or indeed of the mysteries that would be created by such a text. Barring any new discoveries, the surviving texts are all that we have, and they have served historians well over the centuries.

The surviving source material is usually divided into two general groups, the first of which is frequently referred to as the 'Vulgate Tradition' (or derivatives thereof). The term does far more harm to these sources than is probably justified: they present a popular tradition and are represented by Diodorus, Curtius, Pompeius Trogus (in the epitome of Justin) and Plutarch. It is not true to say that these sources are anti-Alexander, but they certainly are not as sympathetic to Alexander as the other tradition, that represented by Arrian.

Of the many contemporary writers on Alexander, none have survived intact. Of the five narratives that do survive, Diodorus is the earliest. Diodorus Siculus was a Greek from Sicily, active in the first century BC, and author of a forty-book history that he called the 'Library of History'. Of this great work, book seventeen deals with the career of Alexander. Diodorus is justly criticized by modern authorities for being an uncritical compiler of information: he also has a tendency to play with dates, and to move events from one year to another in order to fill a time gap and even out events. Diodorus had a tendency to use a single primary source for each book, and in book 17 this was Cleitarchus: he did, however, take information from other writers where appropriate, such as Ephorus, Apollodorus, Agatharchides and Timaeus. Some of his passages are almost identical to the corresponding passages in Curtius, taking into account differences in the Greek and Latin. The size of his work means that frequently he preserves some material that goes unrecorded in the other surviving sources.

Much like Diodorus, Pompeius Trogus wrote a world history, but, unlike

Diodorus, little survives. Trogus was a Romanized Gaul originally from Vasio and, like the rest of the vulgate, used Cleitarchus heavily, although he also relied upon Timagenes. One of the main reasons that Trogus does not survive is the success of the much abbreviated, and evidently of far poorer quality, epitome of Justin.

Quintus Curtius Rufus wrote in the second quarter of the first century AD. He was a Roman, writing in Latin, and was himself an active politician, having held public offices under both Tiberius and Claudius. Curtius wrote his history of Alexander in ten books, of which the first two are now lost, and what remains contains *lacunae* in places (the end of book five and the beginning of book six, plus large parts of book ten). Curtius also primarily used Cleitarchus, but sensibly added many details from Ptolemy and others.

Plutarch was a famous biographer who wrote a series of parallel 'lives' in which every Greek was paired with a Roman counter-part; Alexander being paired with Caesar. All of Plutarch's lives survive, bar two: Epaminondas and Scipio. Plutarch wrote towards the end of the first century and the beginning of the second century AD. Plutarch was a Greek, originally from Chaeronea, but he had also being granted Roman citizenship. The primary problem with Plutarch is that he was writing biography and not history: he usually favours stories that illustrated some character trait even if the historicity was dubious; such as the taming of Bucephalus episode. Whenever Plutarch is cited, it is the *Life of Alexander* that is referred to, unless otherwise stated.

Arrian's narrative is generally, and correctly, regarded as the most reliable of the surviving sources. Lucius Flavius Arrianus (Arrian) was a Greek from Nicomedia in Bithynia. The specific date of his birth is nowhere attested, but since he was consul in AD130, he was most likely born around AD85. Although Arrian gained Roman citizenship (during the Flavian period as his name suggests), he was first and foremost a Greek, writing in Greek and primarily for a Greek audience. In his early life he was a pupil of the great Stoic philosopher, Epictetus, but his *Anabasis* shows little or no bias in that direction. In his adult life, Arrian was a significant figure in the Empire: along with the consulship he was also made governor of Cappadocia by Hadrian and commanded two Roman legions. In terms of content, Arrian was no Thucydides, but he did choose good sources, even if his reason for the choice was dubious at best (Arrian 1.preface). Arrian's primary sources were Ptolemy and Aristobulus, both of whom served with Alexander; unlike the vulgate primary source, Cleitarchus. Arrian's history is generally regarded as being the most reliable, but it should not be used to the exclusion of other data, be it other literary sources, archaeology, numismatics or some other form of evidence. Taken as a whole, we have more information on Alexander than most historical figures; but the evidence is frequently open to considerable interpretation: therein lies the job of the historian. When Arrian is cited in this work, it is always the *Anabasis* that is referred to, unless otherwise stated.

One final note; this book is intended primarily for interested amateurs and students of ancient history; although one would hope that academics may find value in it also. Although this work is of an historical nature, its primary purpose is not source analysis, although this has been undertaken where necessary. Any remaining errors and omissions are, of course, mine alone.

Chapter 1

Macedonian Heavy Infantry

—₥—

Developments in Greek Warfare

In traditional Greek warfare, until the Peloponnesian War, a phalanx was a heavily-armed mass of infantrymen who fought as a coherent body. They wielded spears in their right hands and carried a large shield in their left. This led to the tendency described by Thucydides for men to move not only forward, but to the right as well, in order to gain greater protection from the shield of the hoplite stationed in that position.[2] The hoplites that fought in these phalanxes were relatively untrained, being citizens of the various city-states who were pressed into service as situations demanded. The hoplite phalanx was therefore a relatively inflexible body, mostly incapable of complex manoeuvres, although the actions of the Athenian hoplites at Marathon would tend to suggest that this was not always the case.

The Peloponnesian War represents a watershed in Greek military, social and political history. It lasted from 431-404 with the chief protagonists being Sparta (the great land power), and the naval empire of Athens. The length and brutality of the conflict transformed Greek warfare from a small scale affair, often involving consenting protagonists, into a year round and entirely more dangerous situation. During hoplite battles, each side essentially had to agree to engage in combat. A suitable plain had to be selected as hoplites could not operate across broken ground easily, due to their lack of training. Furthermore, the generals had to deploy their hoplites so that their tendency to drift to the right – as noted above – did not take them into rough ground, or cause them to miss the enemy completely as both sides had the same tendency to drift. If this deployment was impossible, a commander could refuse to offer battle.[3] With these considerations in mind we can see that a battle effectively had to be agreed upon beforehand. It was also considered unsportsmanlike to pursue a fleeing enemy, and the battle itself was perhaps more akin to a giant rugby scrum than one of Alexander's battles.

The Peloponnesian War's effect upon the Greek world must have been similar to that of WWI on Europe. It became apparent that the old way of doing things no longer worked and new tactics were needed. Flexibility became the order of the day and Philip immediately grasped this during his time as a captive in Thebes. This is also, evidently, something that he impressed upon Alexander at an early age.

Philip

When Philip II, the father of Alexander the Great, succeeded to the throne of Macedonia in 359, he inherited a kingdom beset by enemies on all sides and on the verge of collapse. The previous king, Perdiccas III had been killed in a disastrous battle against Illyrian invaders, led by Bardylus. The Macedonian army was comprehensively defeated and the infantry, such as it was, was crushed. Philip immediately recognized that, although Macedonia was in a weak position, the inability of the city-states to unify against him would be their downfall. He also saw that in order for Macedonia to become the dominant, significant military power, reforms were required, particularly of the infantry. In this belief, Philip was certainly influenced by his years as a hostage in Thebes during which time he saw the training and development of the Theban Sacred Band, along with its devastating effectiveness on the battlefield. Within the first year of his reign he had defeated the Illyrian threat and secured Macedonia's borders. Philip achieved this remarkable feat in a number of ways, not all of them military: he was much admired and renowned for his political shrewdness; his seven recorded wives, many of whom came with a new peace treaty, are a testimony to this.

Macedonia had always been renowned for having some of the finest cavalry in the Greek world, but it had never been a significant military power until the point at which it developed an equally strong body of infantry. It therefore seems appropriate to begin by examining the origins and composition of this newly formed force.

The men that comprised the Macedonian heavy infantry are almost exclusively referred to collectively as the 'phalanx' by both ancient and modern authors. The adoption of this term is partly due to convenience and partly due to a lack of understanding on the part of some as to the tactical role of the heavy infantry. Throughout this work I have tried to avoid using this generic term, simply because in the strictest sense it should not apply to the Macedonian *pezhetairoi*; at the very least we can say that it is misleading. In reality the *pezhetairoi* were essentially an evolution of the standard phalanx and more akin to Iphicratean peltasts than a traditional hoplite phalanx.

The term *pezhetairoi* is extremely rare in ancient literature. Its only occurrence outside of the period of Philip and Alexander is in Plutarch (*Flam.* 17.8); the term also occurs infrequently in Arrian (he is the only Alexander historian to use it), for example at 1.28.3; 7.2.1; and 7.11.3, and the term seems to refer to the heavy infantry battalions (*taxeis*), excluding the hypaspists.

The Origins of the *Pezhetairoi*

At some point in time it seems clear that the peasantry of Macedonia were organized into an infantry body that was recruited territorially. Anaximenes tells us quite clearly that at some point the infantry were given the title *pezhetairoi*, a term which translates as 'Foot Companions', effectively making them equal in status to the Companion Cavalry. This was an important development in the heavy infantry as it gave them status, vital in forming a bond with the new king: they would no longer be considered 'cannon fodder'. Theopompus defines who the *pezhetairoi* were, and how they were recruited; these two fragments of source material are both crucial to an understanding of the origins of the Macedonian heavy infantry and will be referred to frequently.[3]

These two fragments unfortunately do not present us with a coherent picture; Anaximenes calls all of the Macedonian infantry *pezhetairoi*, whilst Theopompus believes them to have been picked troops, a bodyguard to the king and not front line infantry. Anaximenes attributes their creation to Alexander, although he does not make it clear precisely *which* Alexander he is referring to, whereas Theopompus makes no statements as to their origins. What can we draw from these two accounts? Were they even talking about the same thing? And who was the Alexander that Anaximenes referred to? The general tendency among scholars has been to accept the testimony of Anaximenes and reject Theopompus where there are contradictions, but this still leaves open the question of which Alexander is meant. Some scholars have claimed that Alexander II must have been the king Anaximenes is referring to, although the brevity of his reign, only one year from 369-8, would tend to eliminate him from such serious reforms. That is, if we assume that the reforms Diodorus mentions occurred at the same time as the creation of the *pezhetairoi*; he also attributes the introduction of the phalanx formation and the sarissa to Philip II, but says nothing about the *pezhetairoi* as such. Diodorus and Anaximenes can only be reconciled if we assume that Alexander II conceptualized the new force and Philip II actually created it. The belief that Philip II was the originator of the *pezhetairoi* has had some significant scholarly proponents.

It could be argued that the Alexander Anaximenes is referring to must be Alexander I; but this would mean dismissing any possibility that it could be Alexander II largely because it would mean that if it were Alexander II, then the reforms made by Archelaus mentioned in Thucydides would be reduced to nothing.[4] This argument, however, is unsound as it relies upon a dubious interpretation of Thucydides and ignores the evidence of Polyaenus and Xenophon, both of whom tell us clearly that even as late as the early fourth century, Macedonia still possessed no properly trained or equipped infantry forces.[5] This would be borne out by the defeat of Perdiccas III's infantry by the Illyrians before Philip II ascended the throne; they were clearly not a well-trained, coherent or organized body of infantry.

Demosthenes, in the *Second Olynthiac*, makes a clear distinction between the privileged position occupied by the *pezhetairoi*, and the mass of the Macedonians who derived no benefits from Philip's policies: according to Demosthenes that is.[6] Demosthenes was, of course, famously anti-Macedonian, and strongly opposed to Philip and later Alexander. Alexander even demanded the surrender of Demosthenes upon the final defeat of Athens, but later retracted the request. If we accept this argument, the conclusion would be that the *pezhetairoi* were not the whole body of infantry that Macedonia possessed, but a select body of guards, equivalent to the *hetairoi* cavalry; and that it is the creation of this body to which Anaximenes referred. If this theory were correct then it was this original unit of guards which was expanded and evolved into the *pezhetairoi* that we recognize from the reigns of Philip and Alexander, and that was so integral to their success on the battlefield. This theory satisfies Theopompus who states that the *pezhetairoi* were a select group of infantry who acted as a royal bodyguard, but does not satisfy Anaximenes, who stated that Alexander gave the name to the majority of his infantry.

Theopompus could have been referring to the *pezhetairoi* as he knew them in the late 340s; if this were the case, then Theopompus' claim that they were an elite group and not the entire body of Macedonian infantry is reasonable. If this is correct then the only way to reconcile the two passages is to assume that the Alexander being referred to is Alexander III, and that the reform was not a significant military one, but that Alexander simply widened the use of the term *pezhetairoi* to include all members of the heavy infantry except for the hypaspists, at the same time widening the use of the term *hetairoi* to include all of the Macedonian cavalry. This would have had the effect of bonding the troops more closely to the person of the king and of slightly reducing their regional ties and the ties to their commanding officers. Alexander's position at the start of his reign was a comparatively insecure one – for evidence that he relied heavily upon the support of Parmenio and his family, see later. This was both a positive step for Alexander's army and a necessary one for him; at the start of his reign he was heavily indebted to Parmenio and his family for their support at the time of Philip's assassination. This was the first step in removing their stranglehold on the throne, a process that would culminate in 330 with the murder of Parmenio and his only surviving son, Philotas.

With regards to the origins of the *pezhetairoi*, the most reasonable argument is that at some point in history, perhaps the reign of Alexander I, an elite group of infantry was created, whilst at the same time the main body of infantry was also trained and equipped in a similar or identical manner, and that it was during the reign of Alexander III that the term *pezhetairoi* was expanded in use to include all of the phalanx infantry. Alexander III was therefore simply changing the nomenclature and status of existing troops rather than instituting some major reform. Alongside this, however, we should note that the reforms of Alexander I evidently did not bring with them significant improvement to the infantry, as demonstrated by the Illyrian disaster. The major advances in effectiveness and efficiency began with Philip II and progressed into Alexander's reign.

What then happened to the original *pezhetairoi* after Alexander? Whichever Alexander that may have been, he expanded the use of the term to include all of the Macedonian heavy infantry. It would be logical to assume that their elite status and special relationship to the king would continue to be recognized in some way, and that they would not simply have been absorbed into the phalanx along with the rest of the heavy infantry. It further seems likely that the pre-existing elite infantry unit was now given the name 'hypaspists' with which we are so familiar from the pages of Arrian. Alexander, as with his father, was always shrewd in his dealings with the army; they both recognized that it was through control of the army that they were allowed to rule. Alexander's sensitivity towards the army, and their love for him, can be demonstrated by their willingness to march from Macedonia to northwestern India, a journey of incredible hardships lasting some eight years from the crossing of the Hellespont in 334 to the mutiny on the Hyphasis River in 326. The difficulties did not end there however, as Alexander decided to take a circuitous route back to Babylon via the Makran Desert, many thousands of miles, with virtually no sign of unrest from them. Only twice did he fail to maintain control of the army. The first time at the Hyphasis River, the modern Beas in northwest India, in 326 when Alexander wanted to press on into India to reach 'Ocean': after three days of sulking, Alexander declared that the omens were not favourable and they would turn back. The second time was in the late summer of 324 at Opis when the Macedonian core of the army, the heavy infantry, felt (perhaps rightly) that they were being replaced by oriental troops and that they were losing their privileged status; a complaint that is key to understanding how Alexander maintained control so effectively for so long.

Creating the Army

Now that we have seen the origins of the *pezhetairoi* we should turn to the question of their training and how they were persuaded to fight with such ferocity and dedication through almost countless battles.

In order to create an army, civilians need to become militarized; this was as true in the ancient world as it is today. Throughout different periods of history this process has involved a number of fundamental elements, these have included: the wearing of a uniform; uniformity of equipment amongst individual units; the swearing of an oath; training designed to engender conformity and solidarity; participation in social events; and the playing of competitive games. The creation of the Macedonian army showed many of these classic features: a uniform was probably worn; combining this with conformity of offensive equipment amongst the leading units of the army would have led to considerable uniformity of appearance. This conformity would certainly have existed within the heavy infantry *taxeis*, the hypaspists and the Companion Cavalry. It is likely that there was a certain amount of conformity of equipment within other units, but the wearing of a uniform amongst, for example, the mercenaries, is unlikely. From the point of view of the enemy, however, it was almost exclusively the Macedonian units that were in the front line, all similarly equipped. To exactly what extent Philip and Alexander attempted to create complete uniformity of dress and defensive equipment is far from clear. The historical sources mention little on this subject and the pictorial evidence is too limited to decide the point. Questions such as a possible change from the use of the Phrygian helmet to the Boeotian within the cavalry, the usage of the *pilos* helmet within the infantry, and even the use of the Macedonian star symbol on shields, are all open to debate. All we can say is that there was probably considerable, if not complete, uniformity of dress and equipment amongst the leading units of the Macedonian army. The very way that the Macedonian heavy infantry operated strongly implies that they had identical weapons if nothing else. With the sarissa, essentially a pike, being the primary offensive weapon, it was vital that no gaps appeared in the wall of spear tips. The sarissa, as we will see later, was an offensive weapon and the heavy infantry were a strike force. The heavy infantry were not a defensive unit and if a gap appeared in the spear wall, either through poor training or lack of equipment, the *pezhetairoi* would never have been as operationally successful as they were.

The swearing of an oath to the king was also a feature of the training of Macedonian troops. The training programme itself was particularly rigorous, a revolution in fact; nothing quite like it had been seen in the ancient world before this time. Diodorus describes it as follows:[7]

'having put their military organisation on a sounder footing and equipped the men with appropriate weapons of war; he held unremitting exercises in full kit as well as competitive exercises.'

Polyaenus gives us a little more information:[8]

'Philip used to train the Macedonians before they underwent dangers to march with full kit often three hundred stades carrying at one and the same time helmets, shields, greaves, pikes, and, as well as their weapons, provisions and utensils for their daily fare.'

Frontinus tells us that the stamina produced by such a training programme was quite deliberately used by Philip to wear down his opponents at Chaeronea; although from what little we know of Chaeronea it appears to be tactics and training, rather than stamina that were the primary factor in the Macedonian victory. Philip opened the battle by leading his right wing against the Athenians, shortly after that he feigned retreat and the Athenians rashly pursued. At a prearranged signal the Macedonians counter-attacked and won the day. Thus we can say tactics and training were both key to victory. It is surprising the Athenians fell for the ruse given that it was very similar to their own tactics at Marathon. Alexander clearly understood well the importance of the training principles that his father had introduced: at the very beginning of his reign Diodorus tells us that he ordered his army to undertake regular manoeuvres. After the campaigns at Miletus and Halicarnassus, Alexander spent time putting his troops through a rigorous training programme, and when 30,000 Persian youths were to be incorporated into the army they were ordered to be trained in the Macedonian way of war and with Macedonian weapons.[9] The efficiency of what this system produced is best described by Curtius:[10]

'With attention fixed on the nod of their commander, they have learned to follow the standards and keep their ranks; what is ordered they obey to a man. When it comes to standing fast, executing enveloping manoeuvres, running to the wing, changing battle order, the soldiers are every bit as skilled as their leaders.'

This extreme discipline has been called a form of 'corporate unity', a feeling that would have been reinforced by ceremonial parades in full battle order, and further reinforced by the use of the terms 'Companion Cavalry' and 'Foot Companions', the latter of which Alexander had expanded in meaning to include all of the Macedonian heavy infantry, rather than simply an elite bodyguard, as we saw earlier.[11] Consistently throughout his career Alexander shows himself to be an extremely astute commander, not just in field operations but during 'peacetime' too. Alexander's much discussed rivalry with his father did not blind him to the major steps forward the Macedonian army made under his kingship. Alexander should be commended for recognizing these benefits and continuing the reform programme.

This solidarity was further reinforced by what amounted to the playing of team games; hunting was a particular favourite amongst the Macedonian elite. The scene depicted in tomb II at Vergina probably shows a royal hunt and gives a good illustration of this preoccupation, one which can be amply supported by the sources. The conspiracy of the pages occurred after a royal boar hunt, for example; and whilst in India, Alexander took part in the hunting of elephants. Alexander won great personal renown by personally hunting and slaying a lion, during which episode Plutarch links the ethos of hunting with that of the warrior. The hunting of less fearsome quarry was also undertaken; apparently the act of hunting was considered enjoyable in itself, even if the animal being hunted was of no threat to the hunter.[12]

Highly organized competitive games were also played relatively frequently throughout Alexander's reign. It is by no means surprising that they tended to be played at critical junctures during the campaign when group solidarity needed to be reinforced, or when there was some other pressing psychological need. Soon after the crossing into Asia Minor, when the army was visiting Troy, Alexander held a competitive race with certain of his companions in honour of Achilles.[13] Whilst in India, after the army had refused to follow Alexander any further, he was presented with an acute problem of how to restore solidarity and repair the psychological damage the army's refusal had caused; part of this process was again to hold competitive games. Games are frequently referred to on important occasions in Arrian; for example: after the capture of Tyre (2.24.6); after the capture of Memphis (3.1.4); after the capture of Susa (3.16.9); after the capture of Zadracarta, the main city in Hyrcania (3.25.1); after founding a new city (4.4.1); at Taxila (5.8.3); after the battle of the Hydaspes (5.20.1); after escaping the Gedrosian desert (6.28.3); at Ecbatana (7.14.1); and at Hephaestion's funeral (7.14.10). Even during less stressful times games played an important role in creating and maintaining the army's spirit: Plutarch tells us of Alexander and his Companions playing some kind of ball game together, and it is clear that banquets would often be punctuated by contests or games of one kind or another.[14] The same can be said of armies of almost all periods of history; during 'down time' the playing of competitive sports has had a key function of maintaining morale as well as fitness.

A further important factor in the creation of an effective army is its desensitization to violence; this comes either naturally because of the society from which the individuals originate, or is imparted artificially. In this regard the Macedonians were almost uniquely positioned: even during times of peace, which were rare, they lived a vigorous outdoor lifestyle which was not conducive to the development of more delicate sensibilities.

Further to this, decades of practically ceaseless warfare must have left them almost totally desensitized to violence, a sadly desirable quality when forging an army.

The final factor essential for creating an army was leadership. The leadership provided by both Philip and Alexander is legendary, and is still capable of inspiring us today; but this is far from the whole story. We should not forget that quality leadership was spread liberally throughout the army. Whether Alexander's officers were new or inherited from Philip, they were generally of the highest quality; men like Parmenio, Perdiccas, Coenus, Cleitus and Ptolemy. It is clear that Alexander took great care in selecting and training his officers; time that was evidently well spent. Alexander appears to have instigated a policy similar to the SS, in that an individual should be capable of performing the role of the next-man-up in the command structure; this ensured maximum flexibility on the battlefield. These talented Macedonian officers are often, unsurprisingly, overshadowed by Alexander in the sources; but they are praised by Curtius for their bravery during the battle of Gaugamela.[15]

Organization – The Commanders

The traditional hoplite phalanx possessed a single individual commander; this is almost certainly not true of the Macedonian heavy infantry. Each *taxis* was capable of operating independently or in conjunction with other units; for this reason each *taxis* had an individual commander. There is, however, one reference in Arrian during the battle of Gaugamela where he implies a single overall commander. Whilst giving the detailed dispositions of the Macedonian centre he states that 'Craterus commanded all the infantry in that sector', these would have all been *pezhetairoi*. Even if it is the case, however, that the Macedonian heavy infantry had a single overall commander, the position was almost certainly nominal, with the real power lying in the hands of the individual *taxis* commanders or *taxiarchs*.

The Macedonian heavy infantry were a highly-trained professional force; they were extremely flexible and capable of fighting on any terrain, as they repeatedly demonstrated throughout Alexander's career. The *pezhetairoi* were organized into six distinct *taxeis*, each having its own *taxiarch*. Each individual *taxis* could be used as a separate tactical unit, or be grouped together with other *taxeis*, or other units, to form what the Wehrmacht would have termed *kampfgruppen*. Given that the Macedonian heavy infantry probably possessed no overall commander, it is clear to see that the Macedonian *pezhetairoi* represent something of an evolution from the standard phalanx. They were, in fact, far more like a modern army and it is this that has prompted modern authors to discuss Philip's 'New Model Army'.

The army of invasion contained six *taxeis* of heavy infantry and three of hypaspists, totalling 12,000 men. Each *taxis* had a nominal strength of 1,500 men, giving a total of 9,000 *pezhetairoi* with the invasion force. Diodorus tells us that an equal number of infantry (12,000) were left behind in Macedonia with Antipater; he also records 1,500 cavalry as remaining behind.[16] We are not explicitly told but the obvious assumption is that there were 9,000 *pezhetairoi* and 3,000 hypaspists, the same as there were with the invasion force. The very size of the force left in Macedonia speaks of the unstable political situation that Alexander left behind. Revolt was never far away, but surprisingly only actually occurred once, in 331, when king Agis of Sparta organized a rebellion that was put down by Antipater. Sparta was not part of the League of Corinth, and thus not directly under Macedonian control. His rebellion was eventually put down, but not easily. If Memnon of Rhodes, a mercenary commander in Persian employ, had lived long enough to put into effect a Persian plan for a naval invasion of Greece, the history of Alexander's reign, and his legacy, would have been significantly different.

During Alexander's early career, his major battles were conducted largely using the Macedonian core of his army; the Battle of Gaugamela was the first instance where Alexander needed every available man, and is therefore something of a fixed point in analyzing the army. It is also the most detailed breakdown of the Macedonian order of battle that we have. We know for certain that there were six *taxeis* at Gaugamela: all are named by Arrian and can be identified by the name of their commander. He states that after the Companion Cavalry, and moving from right to left, came the heavy infantry, as always led by the hypaspists commanded by Nicanor. It is interesting to note that Arrian describes these as shock troops, not as being primarily defensive as is usually assumed of the so-called heavy infantry. Following these three *taxeis* was Philotas, who took general control of the right side of the line, but his location is unspecified. The *pezhetairoi taxeis* were commanded by Coenus, Perdiccas, Meleager, Polyperchon, Philippus (Amyntas) and Craterus. Amyntas, although named, was not present at the actual battle; he was away recruiting in Macedonia. Who actually commanded his *taxis* is far from clear: Arrian names Simmias, the brother of Amyntas, instead of Philippus or Amyntas, but he is the only source to do so. Curtius and Diodorus name Philippus son of Balacrus. The error is likely to be Arrian's and the commander was almost certainly Philippus.[17] Both Simmias and Philippus, however, are obscure to say the least: Philippus is never mentioned again, whilst Simmias only reappears during the plot of Philotas. Either way it is not critical.

The vulgate sources name Philippus as the temporary commander. Amyntas died in Drangiana and his brother, Attalus, was given his command. Meleager, Polyperchon and Attalus all outlived Alexander and maintained their commands until his death; they may therefore be regarded as fixtures. But, between the assault on the Persian Gates and his return from India, we are given the names of six other *taxiarchs*: Alcetas, Antigenes, Cleitus the White, Gorgias, Peithon and Philotas. We also know that three of the original *taxiarchs*, Craterus, Coenus and Perdiccas, were given promotions to various other positions before the return from India. What may be regarded as another 'fixed point' was the Battle of the Hydaspes: here there are clearly seven *taxeis*.[18] How do all of these names fit together? It could be argued that there were in fact nine or ten *taxeis* in India, but there is no positive evidence of reinforcements from Macedonia arriving after 330, and therefore there could not have been the increase in numbers required to create another two or three *taxeis* after the Battle of the Hydaspes as would be required by this theory, unless we assume significant numbers (4,500) of oriental troops being allowed into the *pezhetairoi* at a very early date. The additional names can probably be accounted for as being temporary commanders such as Simmias (or Philippus or Aristobulus: whichever theory is correct they were certainly temporary *taxiarchs*) at Gaugamela. Let us now look at each of the *taxeis* individually to discover how many there were and who were the commanders.

There were three *taxiarchs* who remained in their positions until after the death of Alexander. As mentioned above, these were Meleager, Polyperchon and Attalus, and they therefore require no further comment.

Perdiccas' *taxis*

Perdiccas' *taxis* is not mentioned again after the Battle of Gaugamela and we know that he was promoted before the campaign in Sogdiana; his *taxis*, therefore, must have been given a new permanent commander and therefore a new name. At the Persian Gates Philotas appears as *taxiarch* and it is likely that this seemingly new *taxis* is that formerly commanded by Perdiccas. This is unlikely to have been an extra battalion because Alexander had not had the time for any reorganization between Gaugamela and the Persian Gates. The only place he received any Macedonian reinforcements was Susa, and we are told specifically that they were incorporated into the six existing *taxeis*. There is, however, a problem: when Ptolemy was detailed to capture Bessus, he was given command of a number of troops that included Philotas' *taxis*; these were the only heavy infantry troops he was assigned. The problem occurs in Arrian: Alexander formed two columns, commanded by Ptolemy and Leonnatus, besides that commanded by himself. Arrian clearly implies that Ptolemy was given two *taxeis*, those of Philotas and Philippus. Philippus' *taxis* cannot have been a heavy infantry *taxis* because there were seven at the Hydaspes and the seventh *taxis*, that of Cleitus, had already been named.[19]

The solution is almost certainly that the term *taxis* was used by Arrian as a utility word, and could refer to units outside of the heavy infantry. This is likely not an error of Arrian's making but one of his sources, some of whom had less understanding of military issues than he did; the problem was, of course, exacerbated by Arrian simply transcribing those sources. Both Philotas and Leonnatus were given two *taxeis*, in Leonnatus' case those of Attalus and Balacrus; this latter is clearly the unit of javelinmen that Balacrus commanded at Gaugamela and the Jaxartes. This campaign was one which required speed of deployment and movement and therefore suggests that no heavy infantry were used in this campaign: the *pezhetairoi* were ill equipped and entirely unsuitable for such an operation. This theory, however, assumes that the heavy infantry were akin to traditional Greek hoplites, which they certainly were not. The heavy infantry, on occasion, did not use the sarissa, but were instead equipped with a regular infantry spear. This fact coupled with their light armour instantly transformed them into essentially light infantry with the kind of mobility and flexibility that would be required on a campaign like the Jaxartes. I believe that there were in fact two *taxeis* involved in this campaign, those of Philotas and of Attalus, and that they would have been equipped as noted above, essentially as peltasts.

Craterus' *taxis*

There was no change in command of this *taxis* until the army reached Bactra. When Alexander set off to suppress the revolt in Sogdiana, he left Craterus in military command of the region of Bactria.[20] After this time Craterus regularly acted as essentially Alexander's second-in-command, often with licence to act independently. It is unlikely that he could have held this new post and retained command of his *taxis*; it must have been given a new *taxiarch*. We know that four *taxeis* were assigned to him in Bactria, those of Polyperchon, Attalus, Meleager and Gorgias. The first three names are fixtures, as already noted, but this is the first time we meet Gorgias as commander of a *taxis*, and presumably it must be that formerly commanded by Craterus as his former troops would more than likely still be under his overall command. When Alexander returned from Sogdiana he sent Craterus to Catanes and Austanes to reduce these two areas. Craterus was assigned four *taxeis* for the task, presumably the same four which he had formerly commanded: they were those formally assigned to Polyperchon, Attalus, Alcestas and 'his own'.[21] 'His own' probably refers to the *taxis* formerly commanded by Craterus, but now under the command of Gorgias. The third *taxis* mentioned was commanded by Meleager and not Alcestas. Alcestas did not gain a command until Gandhara; this is more than likely a simple mistake on the part of Arrian or one of his sources.

Coenus' *taxis*

Coenus was certainly still commanding his *taxis* in Gandhara but was promoted to the command of a hipparchy of cavalry probably at Taxila; a hipparchy which he later commanded at the Hydaspes.[22] His *taxis* must, therefore, have received a new commander. There are three names of *taxiarchs* that we have not accounted for, those of Cleitus the White, Antigenes and Peithon. Who therefore was Coenus' successor? It certainly was not Cleitus as Alexander had Coenus' *taxis* with him in Gandhara whilst Cleitus' *taxis* was with Hephaestion and Perdiccas.[23] Peithon is not mentioned in the narrative until much later; the new commander of Coenus' *taxis*, therefore, must have been his son, Antigenes. The seven *taxeis* at the Battle of the Hydaspes are therefore those of Alcestas, Polyperchon, Meleager, Attalus, Gorgias, Cleitus and Coenus. By this time, as we have just mentioned, Coenus was no longer commanding his *taxis*; he had been promoted to command a hipparchy, his battalion now being commanded by Antigenes. We can be certain that Antigenes did in fact command a *taxis* in the battle, and there is no real alternative to assuming it was that of his father, Coenus, even though the old battalion name was still being used. After the Battle of the Hydaspes, Coenus' *taxis* is named as such only a further two times. It was left behind at the Acesines with Coenus himself shortly before his death and is referred to as Antigenes' *taxis* thereafter.

Cleitus' *taxis*

As mentioned previously, Alexander originally possessed six *taxeis*; Cleitus' was the seventh. It is specifically named for the first time soon after the army crossed the Hindu Kush Mountains, and the origins of the seventh can therefore be dated to Bactra.[24] Alexander took Cleitus' *taxis* with him when he crossed the Hydaspes, along with that of Coenus. Coenus' *taxis* can legitimately be regarded as one of the foremost units of the heavy infantry as it was selected to lead the attacks on both Tyre and Aornus. It is likely therefore, as Alexander picked these two *taxeis*, that the new seventh battalion was not made up of raw recruits. Given that it was one of only two that accompanied Alexander on the treacherous crossing of the Hydaspes River before the battle, during the night and in monsoon rains, we can assume that it was a seasoned *taxis* sent to Asia by Antipater after his defeat of Agis, the Spartan king. Agis led a serious revolt against Macedonian rule, even though the Peloponnese was not directly under Macedonian control. The revolt was subdued after a significant struggle in 331.

On the death of Coenus, which occurred just before Alexander set sail down the Indus, Cleitus was promoted to the command of his hipparchy as noted above, and Peithon (the last *taxiarch* that must be accounted for) took over the command formerly held by Cleitus. This battalion appears under the name of Peithon for the first time during the Mallian campaign.[25] This man is not the same Peithon who was later named as being the son of Agenor, the future satrap of Sind. The Peithon that took over from Cleitus is clearly an important individual. He was given the temporary command of two hipparchies of cavalry as well as his own *taxis* during the Mallian campaign: this was a position of significant power and responsibility that a mere *taxiarch* would never have held as a hipparch was of higher rank than a *taxiarch*, and the former therefore would not have been placed under the command of the latter. At the beginning of his reign, Alexander raised the status of the infantry by conferring upon them the title *pezhetairoi*, or Foot Companions. Although this was intended to raise them in status to the level of the Companion Cavalry, it was clearly still the case that the cavalry were the high status troops as signified by a hipparch being ranked higher than a *taxiarch*. It is most probable that this Peithon was one of Alexander's bodyguards, the son of Craterus, who was holding the interim command of a *taxis* but was in fact no ordinary *taxiarch*.

The evidence therefore seems to support the idea that there were six heavy infantry *taxeis* during the early part of the campaign until the army reached Bactra, at which point a seventh was introduced. Whether Antipater had sent this seventh *taxis* is I think highly likely, but not wholly relevant; the seventh battalion certainly existed, and we can also say with reasonable assuredness that there were never more than seven *taxeis*.

Infantry Equipment

We should begin this section by discussing the principal offensive weapon of the heavy infantry, as this is vital to understanding how the infantry moved and operated and what function they performed on the battlefield. Once we have done this we can explode the myth that they were the 'anvil' in the frequently cited 'hammer and anvil' analogy of the Macedonian army. The principle offensive weapon of the *pezhetairoi* was the sarissa, or pike.

The literary evidence can tell us much about the sarissa. Appian describes the infantry sarissa as a 'long spear', whilst the anonymous Byzantine historian contrasts the 'long spear' of the infantry with the 'spear' of the cavalry; Aelian further contrasts the *dorata* of the peltasts with the sarissa of the heavy infantry, noting that the Macedonians were armed with a much longer weapon. Lucian tells us that the sarissa had a sharp iron blade at the fore and a spike on the aft of the weapon, in order that the pike might be dug into the ground so as to impale a charging horseman or infantryman.[26] The butt-spike also acted as a counter balance, allowing the weapon to be held closer to the aft, enabling more of the weapon to be projected to the front of the infantryman. This ability to hold firm against a charging enemy was extremely important. The view often espoused by historians is that of the Macedonian heavy infantry essentially rolling over enemies like some kind of ancient panzer. This was often the case, but the butt-spike enabled the Macedonians to dig in as the enemy approached to receive a charge, perhaps from cavalry, before resuming their own advance.

Theophrastus, a contemporary source, tells us that the longest sarissa was 12 cubits, or 5.5m; whilst Asclepiodotus adds that smallest pike was not shorter than 10 cubits, or 4.5m. Around 300 BC, not long after the death of Alexander, Cleonymus of Sparta had increased the length of the sarissa to 16 cubits, and in addition to this 16 cubit pike (7.3m) a 14 cubit (6.4m) example was also issued; this was the one which was most commonly used by the later Spartans.[27]

The shaft of the sarissa was made of cornel wood which gave the best combination of straightness, hardness and flexibility; in these respects cornel wood was believed to be superior to all other woods available. Cornel wood was also deemed suitable because of its great abundance throughout the Balkans, and was common as far east as Syria. The lack of such trees further east, coupled with the lack of any evidence of a shortage of sarissas later in Alexander's reign, argues for the tremendous ability of the Macedonian logistics machine to keep the army supplied with everything they needed.

From a brief examination of the literary evidence we can draw a number of conclusions regarding the sarissa: the infantry sarissa was longer than the cavalry sarissa, and longer than the standard spear and javelin; the infantry sarissa was issued in 10, 12, 14 and 16 cubit lengths and was constructed of cornel wood; an iron blade was affixed to the fore of the weapon, and a butt-spike was affixed to the aft to dig into the ground or act as a counterweight.

The visual evidence can provide us with more information. The Boscoreale Mural, which probably depicts Alexander IV, the son of Alexander the Great, his wife Roxanne and his tutor, shows the figure of Alexander IV holding a sarissa, the upper part of which is hidden by the architrave above and behind him. The weapon can be identified as an infantry sarissa because of its evident size, even though much of it is hidden, and from the butt-spike that is clearly visible in the foreground. It is this butt-spike that distinguished it from a cavalry sarissa as this had a large weapon head on its aft point. The shaft of the sarissa appears to be of approximately uniform diameter throughout its visible length. Tightly wound around the shaft at a point closer to the aft than the fore of the weapon is a cord of some unknown material, most likely leather. This cord is undoubtedly a handgrip serving two main purposes: the first to ensure that the user was able to hold the weapon if it became slippery during battle; the second was to define where the weapon was to be held. This essentially ensured that every infantryman carried the weapon in the same position so that each pike projected an identical length in front of, and behind, each individual soldier. This uniformity was absolutely essential for the effective operation of the heavy infantry phalanx; any gaps in the line could prove fatal to the overall cohesion of the *taxeis*, as the sarissa was essentially useless as a defensive weapon. The corded grip is quite distinct from that found on the cavalry sarissa, which consisted of a shoulder strap and wrist-loop.

The Alexander Mosaic is an intriguing piece of evidence. It probably depicts Alexander's final charge at the Battle of Issus, although it could represent the Battle of the Granicus River: it is not necessary to know what the actual battle depicted is in order to interpret it. The figure of Alexander is wielding a sarissa. The weapon is something of an oddity: it possesses a hand grip but no wrist-loop as would be expected on a cavalry sarissa, and is in this regard identical to the weapon in the Boscoreale Mural, which we know to have been an infantry weapon. The sarissa wielded by the figure of Alexander is also quite different from that lying broken in the foreground in front of Alexander. The portion of the mosaic that would depict the shaft of Alexander's sarissa is missing, but the large weapon head, along with the shaft which appears to be both thicker and longer than that of the cavalry sarissa on the ground, strongly suggests that Alexander is being portrayed as wielding an infantry sarissa whilst on horseback. Militarily the wielding of a pike by a cavalryman is next to impossible: it would have been simply too long and too heavy to have been wielded effectively in one hand, and would have been almost as difficult in two. It is also more probable that Alexander would have used his back-up weapon, his sword, rather than pick up a virtually-useless infantry sarissa before charging headlong into the heart of the Persian defences.

The shafts of the sarissas depicted on the mosaic all appear to be of uniform diameter and all possess the same weapon head. They also all appear to be equipped with a small piece of metal, essentially a tube around the sarissa, just behind the weapon head. This tube is of the same colour, and thus presumably the same material, as the weapon head. This tube, hereafter referred to as a fore-shaft guard, is of such a size that it would extend down the shaft to a point roughly equal to the level of the next row of sarissas protruding from the line. Its primary purpose therefore is to prevent sword-armed opponents from hacking the blade off the sarissa and thus rendering the weapon useless. This is a fundamental development in the weapon, and although the tube is referred to here as a guard, its purpose is offensive. Some have concluded that the tube was a coupling-sleeve designed to join the two halves of the sarissa together, therefore obviously assuming that the sarissa was actually a two-piece weapon and not a single shaft. This is an interesting yet highly speculative conclusion as it would be very difficult for any join to be strong enough to hold two very lengthy and very heavy halves of a pike together. The sarissa was very far from being akin to a modern snooker cue, for example. The main attractiveness of this idea would be that the sarissa could be easily dismantled for transport, or that only the front end could be used in difficult terrain: in such circumstances, however, it is far more likely that a standard hoplite spear would be used.

The pictorial evidence for the infantry sarissa provides a level of support for the literary evidence; from the pictorial evidence alone we can conclude: the infantry sarissa had a large bladed spear head on the fore part of the weapon and a butt-spike on the aft; a fore-shaft guard was positioned flush with the weapon head to protect the shaft from being severed by an enemy attempting to force a way past a seemingly impenetrable wall of spear heads; the shaft was uniform throughout its length; there was a (probably leather) grip wrapped around the shaft of the weapon towards the aft, partly designed to ensure the weapon would not slip and partly to ensure that every man wielded the weapon in the same position.

The material remains recovered by archaeologists over the last century can provide us with yet more information. The numbers of sarissa heads, along with spear and javelin heads that have been found, are of sufficient quality and quantity to be able to distinguish between them. The artefacts found at Vergina include the iron parts of both infantry and cavalry sarissas along with hoplite spears and peltast javelins. The ordinary spear found at Vergina in tumulus 68 burial E had an iron spearhead 27.6cm long and 127g in weight with an iron butt-spike of 6.35cm in length weighing 42.5g. The spearhead and butt-spike were found 1.88m apart with some fragments of wood in the intervening space; the ordinary spear therefore can be assumed to be around 2.3m in length and weighing 1.13kg in total. The cavalry sarissa consisted of a double-edged flaring aft blade 50cm long and weighing 536g, and a smaller spearhead of 28cm in length and 267g.

The total length of the cavalry sarissa would have been around 2.75m and would have weighed 1.9kg. The infantry sarissa consisted of a four-sided tapering butt-spike, total length of 45cm and weight 1.04kg and a pointed weapon-head with a large, flaring double-edged blade of length 51cm and 1.22kg weight. It also included the fore-shaft guard, as discussed above.

The fragments of the infantry sarissa found at Vergina can be identified as such for several reasons: the presence of the fore-shaft guard and butt-spike confirms the literary and visual sources; the similar socket diameters of both weapon heads and the fore-shaft guard show they came from a weapon with a larger shaft than the ordinary hoplite spear, javelin or cavalry sarissa; the much greater size and weight of the weapon heads of the pike compared to the lance, spear or javelin.

The physical remains of the infantry sarissa clearly confirm the existence of such a weapon and furthermore confirm the literary and visual sources. The archaeological evidence considered in isolation can tell us the following: the fore weapon head is both longer and heavier than the butt-spike; the fore-shaft guard places even greater weight to the fore of the weapon; both the fore and aft weapon heads of the infantry sarissa are larger and heavier than the corresponding elements of the cavalry lance and the spear/javelin; the similar socket diameter of the weapon heads and the fore-shaft guard show the shaft of the pike to have had a uniform cross-sectional area throughout its length.

Summing up the Evidence

Whilst marching in open order each pikeman occupied a space of four cubits, laterally. The open order was mostly employed for route marching.[28] It is likely that whilst marching the sarissa was not actually carried by the infantrymen, they would have been located in the baggage train and a traditional hoplite spear would have been carried. The open order was also employed in certain combat situations in order to close with the enemy quickly whilst at the same time minimizing casualties from projectile weapons. This was achieved because of the positioning of the sarissa whilst in the open order; the sarissa would have been held vertically, thus deflecting some of the enemy projectiles. This positioning was the easiest way to carry a very unwieldy weapon when it was not actually being used. It could also be employed defensively if the enemy might be expected to use chariots or even carts or wagons.[29]

In close order each man occupied 2 cubits of space: this formation was the standard formation for manoeuvring on the battlefield and for fighting when a broad front was required or when less disciplined troops were encountered.[30] The final formation employed by the Macedonian heavy infantry was the compact order, or locked-shield formation, during which time each man occupied only 1 cubit of space. The compact order was used to engage an enemy which was equally disciplined, or when weight of numbers was more important than frontage; this formation was especially useful when a greater degree of defensive capability was required to combat a charge by infantry or especially cavalry.[31] When wielding the sarissa in both hands it would be necessary to rotate the shoulders so that they would essentially face the enemy; thus a smaller space would be required left and right of each pikeman. Therefore a spacing of 1 cubit could be achieved laterally; it would not realistically be possible for each rank to be closer than 2 cubits to the man in front or behind because the distance the hands were apart on the weapon required additional space, thus 2–cubit intervals were maintained from rank to rank. The closed order formation would have a significantly reduced frontage and was rarely used. A formation such as this could not have been employed during the set-piece battles, especially the likes of Gaugamela where there was serious danger of Alexander being surrounded by a massively numerically-superior enemy. A shorter frontage would have played into Darius' hands; this formation was the exception, but the Macedonians retained the flexibility of its use when situations, be they tactical or topographical, required it.

The Macedonian heavy infantry *taxeis* required exceptionally disciplined rank-depth spacing. Using a 14–cubit sarissa as an example, 4 cubits were taken up by the spacing between the infantryman's hands, and by the weighted rear portion of the weapon up to the butt-spike. This left 10 cubits to project in front of the pikeman. In this case four ranks of sarissas would extend beyond the front rank at 2-cubit intervals, and thus five ranks of sarissa heads would extend towards the enemy for each rank of infantry. The sarissas of the second rank would project two cubits behind those of the front rank, the third rank's sarissas 2 cubits behind that etc. The 2 cubits of each weapon that projected in front of the next rank of weapon heads would be protected by its fore-shaft guard, preventing an enemy from hacking off the sarissa head; the formation would be vulnerable to such a tactic if not for the guard. Projecting towards the enemy, then, was what would have looked like a virtually impenetrable wall of large spear heads. From the perspective of an enemy soldier advancing upon the Macedonians, who were themselves marching slowly and inexorably towards you, the site must have been awe inspiring. How could a soldier, wielding little more than a javelin, get past five ranks of spear tips before he could even engage the enemy? It is of little surprise that enemy infantry rarely stood up to the Macedonians for long. Curtius presents us with an excellent description of the Macedonians at the Battle of Issus. He described the Macedonians as an army gleaming not with gold and silver, but with iron and bronze.[32] They were, without doubt, a thoroughly professional army.

The relative effectiveness of this kind of formation required a high degree of discipline and training in each member of the *taxis*, but most particularly in the front few ranks. This is why the front two ranks were manned by officers who earned a higher rate of pay than the rest, although Curtius tells us that the common soldier was no less skilled than the officers. An obvious parallel with modern warfare is again with the SS; each SS trooper was trained to be able to take up the position of the man ahead of him in the command structure, thus the unit would not suffer from the loss of its commander. The unit did not die if you cut off its head. This was necessary given that the officers were primarily stationed in the front two ranks; attrition amongst that group would have been high. The formation would only work if every sarissa head was positioned correctly in relation to every other sarissa around it; otherwise gaps would form in the front of the line that could be quite easily exploited by any relatively competent enemy; particularly one who employed light armed troops rather than hoplites.

The extreme length of the sarissa was a huge tactical advantage for the Macedonian heavy infantry when first encountering an enemy who was equipped as a peltast or as a hoplite. Several ranks of enemy could be killed before the Macedonians were seriously threatened; it was, therefore, a shock weapon, again proving the 'hammer and anvil' analogy so often stated to be entirely false. Often the enemy infantry would be routed quickly and Macedonian casualties amongst the infantry were usually quite low, only growing in numbers as the battle drew on: this is because it was a weapon that also brought with it serious disadvantages. The very size and weight of the weapon meant that it was extremely difficult to handle, requiring tremendous strength and dexterity. It also meant that crossing broken ground, such as a river, or a march through a forest, was difficult. It is possible that the Macedonians only used the sarissa at the Battle of Gaugamela, given that all other battles were fought on broken ground, making its deployment problematic.

The very nature of the weapon also meant that it provided almost no defensive protection: a short spear or a sword could be employed to some extent to fend off an enemy blow, but not a sarissa. This is precisely why Macedonian casualties would rise significantly if the enemy could withstand the initial charge. If the sarissa were dropped so that the infantryman could use his secondary weapon, a sword, in combat, then gaps in the line would immediately open in the 'wall of sarissas'; thus the main advantage of the weapon, its coordinated use, would be lost. Coupling this with the almost complete lack of defensive equipment (discussed below), I would conclude that the Macedonian heavy infantry were not at all a defensive formation, but were a strike weapon in much the same way as the Companion Cavalry. A 'hammer and anvil' analogy is often employed to describe the Macedonian army, with the Companions as the hammer and the heavy infantry as the anvil. This would imply that the Macedonian phalanx was fundamentally defensive: it certainly was not. If this analogy is to persist then the Thessalian cavalry should be described as the anvil, not the heavy infantry, as it is they who essentially performed a defensive role on the battlefield. Alexander's army was created and designed to attack the enemy; to be an offensive weapon. His mindset was evidently to destroy the enemy as quickly as possible: he had little or no interest in conducting defensive operations, but then, he never had to.

Defensive Equipment

We have a number of literary clues as to the equipment employed by the heavy infantry; Polyaenus tells us that Philip, in order to train his troops, had them march 300 stadia under arms with their helmets, shields, greaves, pikes and also their provisions. The Amphipolis Code generally agrees with Polyaenus' list and states that fines were imposed for the loss of any pieces of equipment: two obols for a protective belt for the lower stomach, two obols for a helmet, three obols for a sarissa or a sword, two obols for greaves and a drachma for a shield; again, as with Polyaenus, no mention of a corslet.[33]

Since the sarissa required the use of both hands in order to wield it, the infantryman could only carry a small shield suspended from the neck and covering his left shoulder. Asclepiodotus is our only source for the diameter and shape of the shield: he tells us that the Macedonian shield was made of bronze and that it was 8 palms in width and not too hollow: this probably means relatively flat, not too concave.[34] There is little doubt that the Greek palm equated to 7.6cm, so the shield was 61cm in diameter; the diameter of hoplite shields excavated at Olympia ranged from 78.7cm to 100cm. It is unfortunate that these small shields are never portrayed in ancient art, but the reason for this is obvious enough: if a depiction of the sarissa-armed infantry did exist then the sarissa would so dominate the scene that the shields would either be left off by the artist as a virtual irrelevance, or it would be completely hidden by the mass of men and sarissas. It has been speculated that the sarissa would not have been the only weapon employed by the heavy infantry; it is possible that they did not use it at the Granicus or at Issus, and that infantry that accompanied Alexander on operations that required speed and endurance would also not have carried the sarissa and small shield. If this is the case then at these times they would perhaps be equipped as regular hoplites, with a spear and hoplite shield. Whilst this theory appears superficially interesting, there is no evidence that Philip or Alexander ever ordered the production of large numbers of hoplite panoplies for the heavy infantry. The expense alone would have been prohibitive, especially early in Alexander's reign when we know that gold was scarce.

The training required for the heavy infantry to have operated with both types of equipment would also tend to indicate that hoplite panoplies were never used. It seems most likely that during situations when the sarissa was inappropriate a regular hoplite spear or javelin would be used, along with the small shield. In these situations they would have acted essentially as Iphicratean peltasts, and may have looked very similar to the Agrianians. The many situations where speed was a primary requirement would themselves imply that relatively little defensive equipment would have been used; a full hoplite panoply would certainly slow them down and sap the endurance of troops far more than carrying the sarissa would. It is further unlikely that the baggage train would be employed to carry vast panoplies of equipment that were not at any given time being used, although we should point out that some would have been carried as the allied Greek infantry were certainly still equipped as hoplites and they would have needed replacement equipment from time to time. We know that Philip placed the greatest emphasis on speed and mobility, to such an extent that he banned carts and severely limited the number of servants that accompanied the army; he allowed only one servant for each cavalryman, and only one servant per ten infantrymen. The troops were expected to carry food for themselves, thus giving the army the greatest possible mobility. It is far from clear if Alexander was quite as strict as

Philip in this regard, but it is likely that he did adopt similar ideas, although the presence, and looting, of the Macedonian baggage train during the Battle of Issus proves the existence of one. Throughout the campaign there were certainly more people that attached themselves to the army as it advanced through Asia. These people would generally have been left to trail miles behind the army; Alexander would not have allowed them to seriously slow his progress. The baggage train would have been directed towards a particular rendezvous point whilst the main body of the army was subduing the region without significant hindrance.

In conclusion, the heavy infantry wore very little armour. In order that mobility be achieved, the weight of equipment had to be reduced: it is usually believed that the mass of sarissas offered a measure of protection, thus rendering the corslet a burdensome and expensive luxury. There was also a financial necessity for reducing the amount of equipment, as Philip and Alexander could equip far more troops with lighter armour than they otherwise could have done, and finances were extremely tight for both. The corslet was not totally abandoned, however: officers tended to be issued with one, partly as a status symbol and partly as a necessity. These officers were then stationed in the front two ranks of each *taxis*, these ranks being in the greatest need of protection as they were the most exposed to the enemy. Thus the heavy infantry achieved the greatest possible combination of defence with mobility and offensive capability.

The Problem of the *Asthetairoi*

There are six instances in Arrian where the correct manuscript reading is *asthetairoi* and not *pezhetairoi*.[35] The word itself occurs nowhere else in ancient literature and therefore begs the obvious question: what are the *asthetairoi*? The word appears on one occasion (7.11.3) in the same sentence as *pezhetairoi* and it can reasonably be argued on this basis that it is not simply another name for the *pezhetairoi*. A similar argument can be applied to the hypaspists: they too are clearly something different. I think that we can argue that the *asthetairoi* are a hitherto unrecognized or unknown unit of the Macedonian infantry. It is clear from the context in which *asthetairoi* is used each time that Arrian is referring to a unit of Macedonian heavy infantry with some special connection to the king and performing no discernibly different function from the *pezhetairoi*. The first reference to *asthetairoi* seems to indicate that there is only one *taxis*, but all later references describe them in the plural, *taxeis*; indeed two passages strongly imply that the total number of *asthetairoi taxeis* is equal to half the total of heavy infantry in the entire Macedonian order of battle. It is interesting to note that three of the *taxeis* that are called *asthetairoi*, those of Coenus, Polyperchon and Alcestas, were originally recruited from the old kingdom of Upper Macedonia. From this it may be possible to infer that *asthetairoi* was a technical term used specifically to denote the infantry from Upper Macedonia. If this were true we can go further by noting that these troops were absorbed into the national army long after the infantry had been organized into regular cadres. On this interpretation of Arrian, *asthetairoi* would be a generic term applied to any unit of heavy infantry recruited from Upper Macedonia, but I do not think this is a valid interpretation of the available evidence.

Another interpretation would be to argue that the *asthetairoi* were not whole *taxeis*, but a subdivision, a *corps d'elite* within each *taxis*. This theory is not wholly convincing: at several places, notably 2.23.2, Arrian clearly seems to be applying the term to Coenus' *taxis* in full, suggesting that the entire *taxis* carried the title, not simply a small elite part of it. The context does describe the storming of the walls of Tyre using assault bridges mounted on ships, so the entire *taxis* could not have taken part, but neither could the entire unit of hypaspists that accompanied Alexander, and they are still referred to using their standard title. Both Coenus and Alexander took as many men with them as they could cram into their ships; there is no hint that these men were a specially selected elite. The fact that standard heavy infantrymen could be used for naval operations like the storming of Tyre is testimony to the level of training required of an infantryman. This is also an example of a situation where they would have been equipped with a hoplite spear and certainly not with the sarissa.

The real solution to the *asthetairoi* problem, however, is rather different from those above. We can clearly see from Arrian that during the siege of Tyre when Arrian makes his first reference to the *asthetairoi*, there is clearly only one unit that is described as such, that of Coenus.[36] At Issus, Coenus' *taxis* had been promoted from the position it had held within the line at the Granicus, and during both the battles of Issus and Gaugamela it held the position of honour on the extreme right of the heavy infantry, next to the hypaspists. If the *taxis* that occupied the position of honour on the extreme right changed each day, the fact that Coenus' *taxis* occupied this position on both occasions would be a serious coincidence. If this were true, however, there would only be a one-in-six chance of Coenus' *taxis* occupying that position on each of the two days in question, and therefore only a one-in-thirty-six chance of this occurring on both of the two days, making coincidence seem unlikely and thus we can argue that a rotational system was not in operation. Occupying the right hand extreme of the line was always considered an honour, even outside of Macedonia. The finest troops were always stationed there in an attempt to prevent the tendency among hoplites to move towards the right when moving forward. This was because of a natural human tendency to try and gain more protection from the shield of the man stationed to one's right. On this reading, then, the term *asthetairoi* was a battle honour, in recognition of particular bravery, and the fact that they were from Upper Macedonia is incidental. This is supported by the fact that at Tyre it was the only unit of *asthetairoi* in the army at that time that was selected for the most difficult final assault against the city's southern wall.

This argument is strengthened further when we consider that the number of *asthetairoi* units did increase over time to a point where half of the *taxeis* were thus described: if this is the correct interpretation it would be an interesting piece of propaganda on Alexander's part, as it would have the effect of bonding these units even more closely to the person of the king and reduce regional affiliations and loyalties to individual *taxiarchs*. This is something that he wanted and had been attempting to do from the very start of his campaign by introducing the term *pezhetairoi*, or Foot Companions, in the first place. The Macedonian infantry, therefore, consisted of three elements, the *pezhetairoi*, the *asthetairoi* who were also *pezhetairoi*, and the hypaspists whom we will consider next.

Chapter 2

Hypaspists

—⚬—

The hypaspists were among the most capable and heavily worked troops in the Macedonian order of battle, receiving no less than twenty-eight mentions in the pages of Arrian. With this in mind, then, it is perhaps surprising that some of the most basic details regarding this corps are far from certain: these include their origins and organisation as well as their equipment; even their numbers are not directly known. Each of these issues will, therefore, be therefore examined separately.

The Origins of the Hypaspists

The word *hypaspistai*, commonly Anglicized as 'hypaspists', is not a common one in Greek, outside the pages of Arrian. Indeed, amongst the Alexander historians Arrian is the only writer to give the corps this designation; the others tend to rely upon terms like *doryphoroi* and *somatophylakes*, or Latin equivalents like *armigeri* or *custodes corporis*.[37] This fact alone would tend to suggest that the term *hypaspistai* comes directly from Ptolemy, Arrian's main source for military and administrative matters. It is used in the Macedonian dialect to denote 'bodyguard', having lost its original significance of a 'shield-bearer'. It is highly likely that the change of name in the sources is because when a Greek writer was confronted by a highly specialized Macedonian military term he preferred to translate it into something more familiar, like *doryphoroi*.

The origins of the soldiers themselves are a little easier to determine; although they were a fighting elite they certainly were not recruited from any kind of social elite. They were recruited from the same social class as the *pezhetairoi*; that is to say, the peasantry of Macedonia. Unlike the *pezhetairoi*, however, they were not recruited along tribal lines; each hypaspist *taxis* had no tribal or regional affiliations and was therefore connected exclusively to the person of the king; the very name was probably chosen specifically to cement this relationship. Each hypaspist trooper was individually selected for his skill and physique and they received a greater level of training than the ordinary *pezhetairoi*, because far more was expected of a member of the king's bodyguard. The king who first instituted the corps of the hypaspists was, in all likelihood, Philip II at some time after 356. They were, therefore, still a relatively new creation at the time of Alexander's accession in 336. The fact that they had no regional affiliations and were chosen men acted to bind them to the king and ensure their loyalty, something that was paramount in Alexander's mind.

The hypaspists were the elite units of the Macedonian heavy infantry and as such they always occupied the extreme right of the infantry line during set piece battles, this being the position of greatest honour. Their role in battle was to form a cohesive link between the heavy infantry in the centre and the Companion Cavalry. That they were chosen men, the elite of the infantry, was vital in the successful performance of this role. They also acted essentially as Alexander's special forces; any particularly dangerous or important mission, or one involving the creation of secondary columns, would almost always include the hypaspists. The Agrianians can be included in this category too as we will see later.

Hypaspist Equipment

Our lack of knowledge regarding the hypaspists is probably more clearly demonstrated with this most basic question than with any other aspect of this unit. A view that prevailed for some time was that the hypaspists were more lightly armed than the *pezhetairoi*. There were several reasons for this conclusion: representations of soldiers on coins, thought to be hypaspists, wearing no body armour and carrying a spear; the fact that Alexander took the hypaspists with him on forced marches, along with the Agrianian javelin men, whilst leaving the *pezhetairoi* behind to follow at a slower pace; and comparisons between them and the peltasts of Philip V. The main passage in Arrian that can be cited to support the view that the hypaspists were more lightly armed than the *pezhetairoi* is 2.4.3, Alexander's march on the Cilician Gates. In this case Arrian tells us that in order to surprise the defenders Alexander left the heavy infantry with Parmenio and advanced under cover of darkness with the guards (Arrian often uses the term 'guards' to refer to the hypaspists) and the Agrianians. It is dangerous to draw the conclusion that the hypaspists were more lightly armed than the *pezhetairoi* from this passage; Arrian is here drawing a comparison between the column that Alexander took with him and the rest of the army as a whole, not specifically the *pezhetairoi*. I think it likely that, on occasions such as these, Alexander took with him the hypaspists because of their superior training and discipline, and that on such occasions it is highly likely that they would have been equipped with a hoplite spear or javelin and not with a sarissa, as noted above, which would have been a liability whilst marching through mountainous terrain at night.

We may reasonably conclude that, as the hypaspists were stationed to the right of the *pezhetairoi* in the front line at Issus and Gaugamela, they were equipped in a similar manner; their defensive equipment must have been the same because if they were equipped as skirmishers they would have been annihilated in any prolonged frontal assault. We should remember, however, that the heavy infantry, including the hypaspists, were a strike weapon, and not designed for prolonged engagements. The main tactical advantage that the *pezhetairoi* had over enemy hoplites was the sarissa, and I think it further safe to conclude that, at the very least during the set-piece battles, this was also the main offensive weapon of the hypaspist corps.

There is no literary or archaeological evidence that conclusively shows the hypaspists as being more lightly equipped than the *pezhetairoi*. However, the circumstantial evidence from their activities and position during the set-piece battles indicates that they were equipped in a manner that was identical, or at least almost identical, to the *pezhetairoi*: although the lack of direct evidence to support either point of view must be remembered. We can also say, however, with rather more certainty that the level of training the hypaspists received was sufficient to allow them to use a hoplite spear or javelin as their primary weapon as circumstances dictated, and it was at these times that they could be considered as being more lightly equipped than the *pezhetairoi*. It is my belief, however, that on occasion the main body of the heavy infantry was also capable of using a hoplite spear; it is perhaps more their capability of operating in any terrain that truly separated the hypaspists from the rest.

Arrian frequently uses military terms in a vague and imprecise manner, his use of such terms as 'light' and 'heavy' is often contradictory and confused and he cannot be taken as anything more than a general guide as to the equipment of the units involved, and sometimes not even that. At 3.18.1*ff* Arrian classes the Thessalian cavalry as being 'heavy' and the Companions as being 'light'. To the best of my knowledge, however, nobody has taken this passage to mean anything of the sort. Arrian is not the only one culpable for this: modern historians are all too quick to use such terminology too. Although it is, of course, vague to use such terms, they do have a place. With regard to Alexander's army the major difficulty with the use and interpretation of this term comes with the Macedonian infantry units. As we have seen, the *pezhetairoi* are frequently referred to as heavy infantry when, in comparison to a traditional hoplite, they were nothing of the sort. We always have to bear in mind that these terms are relative.

Arrian is not entirely to blame for the confusion, however, as use of such terms in a military context are always rather subjective. Peltasts were lightly equipped whilst hoplites were heavy; the main difference was that the former wore no armour. Since we have seen that the only the front couple of ranks of the *pezhetairoi* wore *any* armour, it would hardly seem plausible for the hypaspists to have served as front line troops with less armour than the other front line infantry, the *pezhetairoi*. Therefore we can reasonably argue that the hypaspists were equipped in a similar, if not identical, manner to, the *pezhetairoi*.

Organization

With regard to the tactical subdivisions within the hypaspist corps, we have virtually no information from our sources. The very fact that there were 3,000 hypaspists is never explicitly stated in any of the extant historians, and is only inferred from the fact that the hypaspists occupied the same frontage as two *pezhetairoi taxeis* at the Battle of Issus. This general confusion has led to speculation that there were in fact three kinds of hypaspist: the 'royal' hypaspists or bodyguards of the king; the actual hypaspist corps; and, after 327 BC, the *argyraspids*, who were evidently new and possibly an elite force. This theory is not the case, however: there was evidently never anything more than the original hypaspist corps of front-line troops.

With regard to the subdivisions within the hypaspists, and on the basis of certain texts, it could be argued that originally the corps was organized into tactical units of 500 men; one of which was the *agema*, meaning 'royal'.[38] Others have argued, by implication at least, that the hypaspists had always been organized into three units of 1,000 men each, the so-called *chiliarchies*. It is certain that at some point the hypaspists were organized into *chiliarchies*, but the passages in Arrian where he cites the term are all in later books; the earliest being at the end of book four.[39] The term '*chiliarch*', i.e., the commander of a *chiliarchy*, does occur in Arrian before book four: during the siege of Halicarnassus, a Macedonian officer called Adaeus is given the title *chiliarch*.[40] There is nothing in the text of Arrian that even suggests that Adaeus was an officer of the hypaspists; other bodies of infantry could well have been organized into units of 1,000 men, the mercenaries for example, and therefore this cannot be taken as proof that the hypaspists were organized in this way any time before the capture of the Aornus Rock.

The key evidence is Curtius 5.2.3*ff.* Late in 331, when the army was near Susa, Curtius tells us that:

> lest the men become slothful through idleness and so relax their minds, he [Alexander] appointed judges and put forward novel rewards to those who entered a contest concerning military prowess. For those who should be judged the bravest were to have the command of 1,000 men each. It was on that occasion that the force was for the first time divided up into this number; for previously they had been in cohorts of 500 men and bravery had not been the yardstick for rewards.

What followed was a list of eight soldiers who received the prizes awarded by the judges; the final verdict apparently was dependent upon the approval of the army and the list of eight names appears in descending order of merit.

Shortly before this contest, 6,000 Macedonian infantry and 500 cavalry reinforcements under the command of Amyntas, son of Andromenes, reached the army.[41] It is possible that within these 6,000 infantry reinforcements were 1,000 or more hypaspists, taking their paper strength to 4,000. If this were true it would further be possible to speculate that the change in corps size also occurred around this time. The victors of the contest, it has been argued, were given the rank of *pentacosiarchs*; thus there would have been 4,000 hypaspists divided into four *chiliarchies* of 1,000 men, each *chiliarchy* being subdivided into two *pentacosiarchies*.

This argument is suspiciously neat and there are certainly problems with it. Arrian strongly implies that the 6,000 infantry reinforcements were only *pezhetairoi* and not a mixture of *pezhetairoi* and hypaspists. There is no evidence in any source that the numbers of hypaspists was ever raised to 4,000. Such evidence as exists tends to suggest that their numbers remained relatively constant at around 3,000: in India (Gandhara) for example, Ptolemy was given command of 'the third part of the hypaspists'; this is far more likely to be one third of three *taxeis* rather than one third of four.[42] We also know from Diodorus that by 318 the hypaspists, now called *argyraspids*, numbered not more than 3,000. By maintaining their number at 3,000, Alexander could present this group as the elite of the heavy infantry, a unit that others could aspire towards.[43]

What can we make of Curtius' narrative? We can probably deduce that Curtius is referring to the hypaspists even though he does not explicitly say this, as we can say that Alexander would not have made such a big issue out of reforming the League of Corinth troops (who were to be dismissed very shortly after this at Ecbatana), nor the mercenaries or Balkan allies; and we have no evidence at all that the organization of the heavy infantry was ever changed in this manner. The question that remains, however, is whether Curtius is to be believed. He is, after all, the only source to mention this reform. I think the answer is in two parts. We perhaps can believe that there was a reform at this time in which the hypaspists were reorganized from *pentacosiarchies* into *chiliarchies*. The reform is very simply stated and there is nothing particularly sensational about it that would make us doubt it. This is not a particularly strong argument, however; all we can really say is that the reform is plausible and there are no grounds to reject it.

The question of the manner in which the reforms took place is an entirely different matter. The *chiliarchs* of the hypaspists were men of great distinction and at least ranked as highly as a *taxiarch* of the *pezhetairoi*. It is virtually impossible to conceive that a man like Alexander would allow anybody, or any process, to make an officer appointment, let alone an appointment to a command (or significant sub-command) of his own bodyguards, one of the elite heavy infantry units in the entire army. One suspects that he would always have the final word in such matters. This desire in part would have come from inheriting an army filled with commanders that were his father's men and not his own, and the years it took to replace those that did not meet with his approval.

One very plausible solution to the Curtius passage is that either in Curtius, or one of his sources, there was a conflation of two separate incidents which both took place whilst the army was at or near Susa. The first was the reorganization of the hypaspists into *chiliarchies* and the consequent appointment of *chiliarchs*; the second was a military decoration ceremony in which men who displayed outstanding bravery in previous campaigns were presented with some kind of awards or rewards. During this ceremony Alexander appointed a panel of judges for this purpose, and rank and file soldiers were encouraged to voice their approval or disapproval of the judges' verdicts; after all there could be no better witness to bravery on the battlefield than the comrades-in-arms of those being rewarded. It is easy to imagine such a situation occurring and it would have been psychologically sound at this juncture, towards the end of the war (as far as the Greeks were concerned, that is!). This kind of ceremony would have been an excellent morale booster, and shows Alexander to be a man who thoroughly understood the psychology of his troops. These awards would have meant little to Alexander in the sense that they were not promotions, but would have meant everything to his troops.

Diodorus appears to be using the same source as Curtius at this point, but his narrative is too vague and compressed to be of any real help. All we can say with any degree of certainty is that at this time the army was reorganized; we are not told which elements, or what the details of these reorganisations were.[44]

This reform took place during the pivotal year of 331, at which time many of the other sections of the army were also reorganized, some new were created, others disbanded. We can only speculate as to the purpose of this reform: the case that is often made for this reorganization is that the reforms were to make the army more mobile, a realization of the changing topography that the army was about to enter. This argument can apply to the Companions whose new sixteen *lochoi* would certainly have been more flexible than their old eight *ilai*, but the reverse occurred with the hypaspists: they went from 500 men to 1,000 men units. It may be that Alexander had come to realize, as the Romans later did when they switched from the manipular to the cohort legion, that 500 men was simply too small a tactical unit to operate independently. If this argument is correct, and I find it extremely plausible, then Alexander had a considerable level of advanced intelligence of the terrain and topography of Bactria and

Sogdiana that he was about to enter. This kind of intelligence is something we seldom have specific reference to in the sources and must glean what we can from extracts and inferences such as this.

Despite a lack of positive evidence, I think it is safe to infer that there were 3,000 hypaspists and that they were indeed organized into three units. Their smaller size than the regular 1,500 allowed for greater operational flexibility, as these were the troops always given the most difficult tasks. This is evidenced by their use on almost every mission that Alexander conducted throughout his career. The standard format was the hypaspists, Agrianians and possibly some other minor units such as mercenaries or Cretan archers. Larger units of 1,500 would have found it far more difficult to cross the mountains at night, for example, or to outflank the defenders at the Persian Gates.

Chapter 3

Macedonian Cavalry

—ɷ—

The following two chapters are devoted to arguably the most important troops in Alexander's order of battle: his heavy cavalry. Every element in the army was trained to undertake a specific role, however small that role may have been, whilst at the same time maintaining the greater tactical flexibility of being able to perform more than simply one task. There seems little doubt, however, that without the heavy cavalry, Alexander's conquests would have been all but impossible. These units provided the main strike force of the army, always the ones expected to make the decisive breakthrough, or to prevent the army from being outflanked. Typically the Companion Cavalry were responsible for achieving the breakthrough, as at the Granicus, Issus, Gaugamela and the Hydaspes, with Parmenio and the Thessalians performing a defensive function on the left wing. The Macedonian cavalry can be divided into two subsections, the Companions and the *prodromoi*, each of which will be dealt with separately. First, however, we will determine the total number of cavalry Alexander had at his disposal at the outset of the campaign in 334.

Cavalry Numbers

Diodorus is the only source that gives us the strengths of individual contingents within the Macedonian order of battle as it crossed the Hellespont.[45] As is frequently the case with Diodorus, his account leaves much to be desired. There are problems in his descriptions of almost every part of the army, not least the cavalry; but with close textual analysis we can eliminate many of them. We are fortunate in this regard that although we have no details of troop strength from other sources, we do have totals; these are listed below:

Source	Reference	Cavalry Total
Livy	9.19.5	4,000
Aristobulus	*FGrH* 138 F 4	4,000
Justin	11.6.2	4,500
Callisthenes	*FGrH* 124 F 35	4,500
Diodorus*	17.17.4	4,500
Diodorus	17.17.4	5,100
Ptolemy	*FGrH* 138 F 4	5,000
Arrian	1.11.3	Over 5,000
Anaximenes	*FGrH* 72 F 29	5,500

For the troop numbers that they provide, Arrian's source was Ptolemy: Diodorus' source was Callisthenes.[46] The total of 4,500 given by Diodorus corresponds nicely with that given by his source, Callisthenes, and by Justin. The actual total of 5,100 in Diodorus corresponds almost exactly with that in Arrian and his source, Ptolemy. The difference of 600 lies with a contingent that Ptolemy/Arrian included but Diodorus/Callisthenes did not. Anaximenes on the other hand gives a larger total than any of the other sources. Given that it is highly likely that the Alexander historians would have had a general tendency to underestimate the size of Alexander's army, as well as its losses, we are probably drawn towards accepting a figure that is towards the highest end of the estimated range, or perhaps a figure even higher still. There was far more glory, after all, in a very small army defeating a considerably larger one.

If we accept as a starting point Arrian's, Ptolemy's and Diodorus' calculated figure of 5,100 as being substantially correct, how do we explain the discrepancies with the other sources? Why does Callisthenes give a figure 600 lower than Ptolemy? It is important to realize at this point that we do not have the actual words of Callisthenes, only Polybius' statement that Alexander possessed 40,000 infantry and 4,500 cavalry for the crossing into Asia. Callisthenes could, potentially, have given two detailed army lists, the first for the army that was mobilized in Macedonia, the second for the army that crossed into Asia. This is, of course, speculation and unverifiable, but I do not think it unlikely that Callisthenes, as the official expedition historian, would give two detailed lists, one list for the army as it left Pella, the other for the army after its safe arrival in Asia Minor, especially if the totals would be different after the incorporation of the

---

* 4,500 is the total stated by Diodorus; 5,100 is the total reached by adding up the strengths he gives for individual contingents.

remnants of the expeditionary force. On this interpretation, Polybius provides us with Callisthenes' first list, not the second, thus missing out a contingent picked up between Pella and the Hellespont; the potentially missing contingent would be the 600 Thracian cavalry.[47] The army did, without doubt, contain a Thracian contingent and it is highly likely that these cavalry would have met up with the army as it crossed through their homeland, rather than travelling to Pella first.

If Anaximenes is in any way correct with his figure of 5,500 cavalry, how can we explain the difference of 400 from Ptolemy? If we accept the idea that Ptolemy gave the army total for the crossing and Anaximenes is giving a total that includes the remnants of the expeditionary force, is it likely that this force consisted of only 400 cavalry? It can almost certainly be assumed that Philip would have realized that his Persian enemies' main strength was in cavalry, not infantry. With this in mind it seems odd that the only cavalry that he sent with the expeditionary force were around 400 mercenary cavalry. Even these are not known directly; their presence is inferred from the fact the they are not present at Diodorus 17.17.4, but are with the army soon after, during the siege of Halicarnassus, and no reinforcements are recorded in the interim. If the expeditionary force did contain only 400 cavalry, then the figures of Callisthenes, Ptolemy and Anaximenes can be made to agree with very little difficulty, simply by assuming that they were the troop totals at different 'stages of the expedition.

Were there only 400 cavalry with the expeditionary force? It is at this point that we first encounter the problems with the *prodromoi*. It is often assumed that Diodorus includes them in his army list. He does indeed use the word *prodromoi*, but actually says '900 Thracian and Paeonian *prodromoi* with Cassander in command'.[48] As discussed below, however, the word *prodromoi* can be a generic term simply referring to 'scouts', or it can specifically refer to a corps of Macedonian light cavalry. In this case I believe Diodorus is using it in the wider sense, meaning scouts without any ethnic association attached.

It could be the case that the 600 Macedonian *prodromoi*, which Alexander undoubtedly possessed, were included in Diodorus' figure of 1,800 Macedonian cavalry.[49] The *prodromoi* were, in all probability, the first cavalry in western warfare to be specifically trained, equipped and employed as scouts. It is certainly true that Diodorus does not call these cavalry 'Companions', but a figure of 1,200 Companion Cavalry (1,800 minus 600 *prodromoi*) is far too low for the roles they performed in set-piece battles, and indeed at other times. We also know that there were eight *ilai* of Companions and that each *ile* consisted, in all likelihood, of 200 troops with the *agema* being of double strength; thus giving a total of 1,800 men. 1,200 Companion cavalry is simply not possible.

If Diodorus is referring to the Balkan light cavalry and not the Macedonian *prodromoi* at 17.17.4, then where were they in 334? I believe it highly unlikely that Philip would have only sent 400 cavalry with Parmenio and the expeditionary force in 336 and no Macedonians at all. The infantry of this force were, in all likelihood, mercenaries. Alexander's Macedonians would have been too valuable to him to send to Asia at this time, although the *prodromoi* may have already been in Asia when the army invaded. They would have been well suited to the type of reconnaissance operations that would have been needed in Asia Minor. If the Macedonian *prodromoi* had been with the expeditionary force too, the 10,000 troops sent to Asia Minor in 336 would have included 1,000 cavalry, and would have been far better equipped to meet and deal with the strength of their Persian opposition. Some small corroboration of this is that the commander of the *prodromoi* at the Granicus was Amyntas, one of the commanders of the expeditionary force in 336. If these assumptions are correct the cavalry forces would look something like this:

Number	Troops	Joined army where?
1,800	Companion Cavalry	Pella
1,800	Thessalian cavalry	Pella
600	Supplied by the League of Corinth	Pella
300	Paeonian *prodromoi*	Pella
600	Thracian *prodromoi*	*en route* to the Hellespont
400	Mercenary cavalry	In Asia
600	Macedonian *prodromoi*	In Asia

On this reckoning the troops that set off from Pella totalled Callisthenes' 4,500; the troops that actually crossed the Hellespont give Ptolemy's 5,100; including the mercenary cavalry gives Anaximenes' 5,500; but the real total of cavalry soon after landing in Asia was closer to 6,100, assuming few losses in cavalry from 336 to 334.

Reinforcements

The first cavalry reinforcements that we hear of after the crossing into Asia are 300 Macedonian horses that joined Alexander at Gordium. Very soon after these first reinforcements, Callisthenes, according to Polybius, has 500 more reaching the army before it enters Cilicia.[50] Arrian tells us of a further group of Macedonian reinforcements that arrived at Susa, but gives no figures. These are in all likelihood the same as those mentioned in both Curtius and Diodorus as having arrived at Babylon; they were, in that case, 500 Macedonian cavalry, along with 6,000 Macedonian heavy infantry.[51] The difference in location is a minor point and is probably a mistake by one of our sources. This would mean that by late 331 Alexander had removed from Macedonia 3,700 native cavalry: 1,800 Companions, 600 *prodromoi* and 1,300 reinforcements. This does, of course, assume that the *prodromoi* were native Macedonians as I have argued above.

It is likely that 500 more Macedonian cavalry would have reached the army in 328/7, at the time the seventh heavy infantry *taxis* was formed. In all likelihood Alexander would have received no more Macedonian reinforcements from this time until his return from India; a period which saw him incur significant losses, to say nothing of those who were left on garrison duty. It should be noted that those most frequently left on garrison duty were mercenaries. Some Macedonians too would have been pensioned off if they were too old or wounded and no longer fit for active service. Casualties are always difficult to determine; along with the general tendency to understate the size of the army, casualties were also underestimated in a deliberate effort to make Alexander's victories seem all the more glorious. This is not simply a problem of the Alexander historians, of course, but of all our sources for almost any period of history. The only occasion where casualties are accurately admitted is the one occasion when Alexander was not present and therefore could not be blamed.[52] Losses in battle would probably have accounted for only a small percentage of the total losses, with disease, starvation and fatigue being more significant factors, particularly during the Gedrosian disaster. There may have been as many as 50,000 casualties for the Gedrosian campaign alone, although the losses amongst the camp followers would have made up the bulk of this number: we can assume that Alexander ensured that what rations there were during this ill-conceived march would have been given to the Macedonians first.

Prodromoi

We should first note, with a certain amount of surprise, that the ethnic origin of the *prodromoi* is far from clear. Frequently Arrian refers to the *prodromoi* with no reference to ethnicity, but at 3.8.1 he includes the Paeonians as part of this unit; at other times, however, he does differentiate the two.[53] Diodorus' army list for 334 does not make the situation any clearer, calling the Thracians and the Paeonians *prodromoi*.[54] Some historians do go along with the evidence of Diodorus, calling the *prodromoi* Thracians and linking them with the rest of the Balkan cavalry, but they are in a definite minority and are almost certainly incorrect. The confusion can, in all likelihood, be cleared up quite simply. The word *prodromoi* translates as 'scouts'; it can thus be used to denote not just a specific unit, but a role or function too. The Balkan horse were undoubtedly light cavalry, as were the *prodromoi*, and thus both could be employed on scouting missions. We can probably assume that any confusion over their ethnicity arises out of the non-technical or non-specific use of the word. Balkan cavalry could act as scouts, but they should not be referred to as *prodromoi* in any specific way. We can, I think, safely assume that the *prodromoi* were Macedonian, as Arrian frequently refers to them together with the Companion Cavalry, whom he also never calls Macedonian. He similarly never refers to the hypaspists or the heavy infantry as being Macedonian, although there can be little doubt on that score, whereas non-Macedonian units are carefully distinguished.[55] Although this is essentially an argument from silence, in this specific instance it is not an unreasonable one. We can go a little further than this, though: the *prodromoi* always seem to have been stationed alongside the Companion Cavalry during the set-piece battles, and were quite separate from the Balkan cavalry, strongly indicating that they were separate units.

Plutarch, in his account of the Battle of the Granicus, tells us that Alexander charged into the river with thirteen *ilai* of cavalry.[56] These thirteen *ilai* were almost certainly the eight squadrons of Companions and five of *prodromoi*. As discussed above, however, *prodromoi* in this passage simply refers to light cavalry; Plutarch is using the word in its non-specific sense. These five *ilai* of *prodromoi* therefore include the single squadron of Paeonians, leaving us four *ilai* of Macedonian *prodromoi*. This figure corresponds nicely with Arrian 1.12.7, where he also gives four *ilai* of *prodromoi*; and later 4.4.6, where he lists four *ilai* of *sarissophoroi*. *Prodromoi* and *sarissophoroi* are in all probability the same troops, just equipped differently for their different roles, the former being scouts, the latter being front-line cavalry equipped with the cavalry sarissa. Plutarch gives no indication as to the nationality of his thirteen *ilai*; they could conceivably have been Thracians or mercenaries, but I believe the above interpretation is the most plausible as it is supported by both Arrian and Plutarch. A total of 600 *prodromoi* seems the most likely; corroboration of this figure is given below.

The *prodromoi* seem to have been amongst the most versatile troops in the army: we should consider them as being the mounted equivalent of the Agrianians in terms of their flexibility and the variety of roles they performed. As discussed above, the word actually means 'scouts', and in this capacity they would often have been sent well ahead of the main army to gain more accurate intelligence of the regions the army was about to enter. They would have been looking not only for the easiest terrain through which the army could traverse, but also for sources of fresh water and supplies; this function was quite simply vital to the success of the campaign. Their ability as scouts is evident by the army's lack of supply problems throughout almost all of the campaign, with a few notable exceptions such as the Makran Desert disaster. Whilst on scouting duty they would have been as lightly equipped as possible, wearing very little armour and carrying a javelin rather than the sarissa. The versatility of these troops becomes apparent when we consider the great set-piece battles. During these battles the *prodromoi* were equipped with the cavalry sarissa, and were then frequently called *sarissophoroi*, or lancers. Their function was to act as anti-cavalry troops and they were deployed in open order; this being necessary in order to prevent danger from the butt-spikes of the sarissa to friendly troops riding behind the front line.

However useful the *prodromoi* were in the early years of the campaign, they were evidently far from essential; we hear nothing of them after the reorganization of the army in 329. It is possible that they were demobilized and sent home, or perhaps left as garrison troops in the east, but it seems far more likely that such fine front-line cavalry would simply have been incorporated into the newly-formed hipparchies of Companion Cavalry discussed below (assuming they were Macedonian). After the reorganization they were no longer required to perform the role of *prodromoi/sarissophoroi* as they had previously; their role as scouts was taken by the increasing numbers of Persian light cavalry that the army was recruiting. Incorporation into the hipparchies meant that they effectively became Companions and in any future set-piece battle they would be stationed alongside the existing Companions as they had been previously; there was, therefore, no distinction between the two after this pivotal year.

Companion Cavalry

The Companion Cavalry were among the most important units in the Macedonian order of battle. They were heavy cavalry recruited from the nobility of Macedonia; 1,800 in number at the start of the expedition. It is unknown if any were left behind in Macedonia with Antipater, but it is almost certain that *some* cavalry were left behind; what they were specifically is unknown. There were originally eight *ilai* (squadrons) of Companions, each 200 strong, one of which was the Royal Squadron, or *agema*, of double strength.[57] It was the role of the *agema* to defend the king whenever he fought on horseback; and when satrapal governors or unit commanders were required they were usually chosen from amongst this group. They were the most trusted and most able of the Macedonian cavalry. The Companions seem to have been organized on a territorial basis. We know of five named *ilai*: those of Bottiaea, Amphipolis, Apollonia, Anthemus and the 'so-called Leugaean *ile*'.[58] There is very little difficulty over the first four of these *ilai* designations; they are areas of Thraceward Macedonia where Philip had established settlements. The exception is the Leugaean *ile*: the name itself presents problems; it refers to no known place in Macedonia, and emendations to the text of Arrian seem to present more problems than they solve. Arrian's qualification, 'so-called', may gives us a clue as to the solution: it may not refer to a specific geographical location at all, but may be a native Macedonian title for the squadron, perhaps a unit recruited from the heartland of Macedonia and thus a much older unit; the other named *ilai* being those formed during the reign of Philip II in newly-settled areas. If this logic is to be followed then it is reasonable to assume that the other *ilai*, of which we know little beyond their existence, could well have come from the heartland of Macedonia as well, and may also, therefore, have had non-territorial names.

The average strength of an *ile* at the outset of the campaign was around 200 men, with the *agema* consisting of 400, giving a total cited earlier of 1,800 troopers. This general organization survived until the army reached

Susa in 331, at which point we see the first of several reorganizations of the Companions. At this time Alexander received reinforcements from Macedonia: these were distributed among the existing *ilai*, but each *ile* was thereafter subdivided into two *lochoi*, under the command of a *lochagos*. This reorganization of the Companions occurred because by 331 there were more Companions than in 334, and the *ilai* were becoming too large to function satisfactorily as individual tactical units. They were, quite simply, becoming too cumbersome and unwieldy.

Hipparchies

In 334 the Companion Cavalry was under the overall command of Philotas, but upon his death in 330 the command was divided between Hephaestion and Cleitus; presumably each being given command of four *ilai*, although we are only told that the eight *ilai* were divided between these two commanders: each commander was also given the title 'hipparch'. It does not necessarily follow, however, that the hipparchies proper were also formed at the same time; this actually came two years later in 328. It has been proposed that after the murder of Cleitus in 328, Alexander took personal command of Cleitus' four *ilai*. This is perhaps supported by the fact that in 327, when the army was divided in the Parapamisadae, Hephaestion and Perdiccas were sent via the most direct route to India with a large force that included four *ilai* of Companions. The remainder of the Companions, those that were formerly commanded by Cleitus, accompanied Alexander himself. This organization imagined by Tarn does not seem likely; Arrian does not say that Hephaestion had sole command of the troops that were sent via the direct route to India, indeed he strongly implies that Hephaestion and Perdiccas had joint command, presumably of the Companions as well as the other elements present. Indeed in 328/7 both Craterus and Coenus were given commands of detachments of troops that included Companion Cavalry, indicating that the command structure within the army was becoming more fluid and less reliant upon a small group of generals.[59]

There are references to hipparchies before the murder of Cleitus in late 328, and these deserve some examination as they may reveal an evolving organisational system.[60] The first reference is in the winter of 334/3: Alexander sent Parmenio to Sardis with 'a hipparchy of the Companions, and the Thessalian cavalry, and the rest of the allied troops and the baggage train'.[61] This could be a reference to a group of *ilai*; a single *ile* of 200 men would be a minor detail compared with the many thousands of other troops that were under Parmenio's command at this point. Alexander's winter campaign in Lycia and Pamphylia shows that very few *ilai* of Companions took part as they receive only a passing mention in the sources, probably because the terrain was not suited to their correct deployment. He sees the eight *ilai* of Companions as being equally divided between Alexander and Parmenio, and therefore the term 'hipparchy' would be used by Arrian to refer to a group of *ilai*, essentially what it means later. Simply because the Companions are seldom mentioned in Lycia and Pamphylia does not of course mean that they were not there, just that they were not used. The tens of thousands of Allied and mercenary troops that Alexander undoubtedly commanded are not mentioned at the Granicus; again this does not mean they were not present, simply that they were kept in a reserve role. The term 'hipparchy' is here almost certainly anachronistically used by Arrian's source. There are a number of occasions where a group of *ilai* is not referred to as a hipparchy before the key date of 328. It is likely that this is not an example of Arrian being scrupulously pedantic, but simply of following the term used by his source.[62]

The second example occurs in Sogdiana in 330: Ptolemy is given 'three hipparchies of the Companions and all of the *hippakontistai*' (discussed below), and charged with the capture of the rebel leader, Bessus.[63] This reference is far more revealing: it is the first mention of the term 'hipparchy' in a passage that definitely derives from Ptolemy. This passage is confusing because, very shortly before this point, Arrian tells of the appointment of Hephaestion and Cleitus as hipparchs; but if there were indeed at least three hipparchies then surely there should have been at least three hipparchs. It is possible that this refers to three 'groups of *ilai*' rather than three individual *ile* with the term hipparchy being again used anachronistically. It is interesting to note that from this time the term *ile* virtually disappears from Arrian's narrative; there could be a gradual reconstruction and reorganisation of the cavalry forces lasting from 331 to 328, when the eight hipparchies emerge seemingly fully formed. I would argue, however, that the hipparchy principle was one that evolved after the murder of Philotas in 330, and the subsequent appointment of two hipparchs, to 328 when we certainly have the eight hipparchies. The murder of Philotas is key to the development and reorganization; it evidently became apparent to Alexander that entrusting such a large group of elite troops to a single individual who seemingly could not be trusted (as with Philotas' father Parmenio) was, to say the least, dangerous. This reorganization and the break-up of commands were partly designed to make the figure of the king the main focus of the army. The reorganization of the infantry to reduce regional affiliations had a similar rationale.

We know then that there were eight hipparchies in 328, but just how many were there at the time of the Indian expedition? No complete list of the hipparchies exists from this period, just as no list of *ilai* exists for the period before 328. We can infer from the sources, however, that Alexander possessed at least eight hipparchies in India. Whilst at the confluence of the Hydaspes and Acesines rivers, Alexander divided the army into four parts (and later five, see below); these were commanded by Craterus, Hephaestion, Ptolemy and Alexander himself. Each of the detachments was given orders to reunite at the junction of the Acesines and Hydraotes rivers. This was done partly to conquer more territory on the journey home, and partly to reduce the food and water requirement for the main army. Each individual section could seek its own supplies from the terrain that it traversed. We know that Alexander had half the Companions during the Mallian campaign, and we can reasonably surmise that this would have included the *agema*, given that they were essentially his personal bodyguard.[64] He also commanded the two hipparchies that we are specifically told about, those of Perdiccas and Cleitus the White; these both being detached for independent operations. When Alexander was at the Hydraotes he still had with him two hipparchies, one of which was commanded by Demetrius. There is no evidence that Perdiccas had rejoined Alexander before the attack on the city of the Malli.[65] 'Half the hipparchies' appear to have been four; just before the assault on the city of the Malli, Perdiccas still had not rejoined Alexander, Ptolemy was fighting elsewhere, Hephaestion was already waiting at the appointed rendezvous and Craterus was in command of no Companion cavalry at all.[66] It therefore seems that there were eight hipparchies along with the *agema*.

There is further evidence for the number of hipparchies: our sources record the names of six hipparchies, the names of the seventh and eighth presumably lost at some point. They were:[67]

Hephaestion	Arrian 5.12.2; 21.5
Perdiccas	Arrian 5.12.2; 22.6; 6.6.4
Demetrius	Arrian 4.27.5; 5.12.2; 16.3; 21.5; 6.8.2
Craterus	Arrian 5.11.3
Cleitus the White	Arrian 5.22.6; 6.6.4
Coenus	Arrian 5.16.3

Although I believe that there were eight hipparchies, along with the *agema*, during the Indian campaign; we can not escape the fact that in 324 we are told of the *addition* of a fifth hipparchy. This would seem to disprove that belief, but it need not. Losses during the Indian campaign and during the ill-fated march through the Gedrosian Desert must have been heavy and it is certainly reasonable to assume that at some point the eight (or nine if we view the *agema* as the ninth) seriously under-strength hipparchies were reorganized into four, and later five. It would seem that hipparchies that were perhaps only half strength were of little tactical use to Alexander; amalgamating them was the perfect solution. It would further seem likely that the initial division into eight or nine hipparchies occurred in 329 or 328, perhaps soon after the death of Cleitus. This again had the further effect of reducing regional affiliations, and changing commanders meant that individuals did not build a loyalty to individual unit commanders; the main focus of the army's loyalty remained Alexander himself.

The reorganization into hipparchies was certainly a serious structural one, and not simply a change in nomenclature or command. With this in mind, why did the reorganization to hipparchies occur at all? Why was it necessary?

Without detailed evidence from our sources on this question it is very difficult to answer with any degree of certainty. Several different ideas have been proposed, all of which carry problems. The reorganization could have been for essentially military reasons.[68] On this interpretation, after the discharge of the Thessalian cavalry, Alexander reorganized his Companions into the eight hipparchies, these were further divided into two *ilai*; each *ile* being further subdivided into two *lochoi*. Since a hipparch was of a higher status than the old *ilarches*, the commander of an *ile*, this would therefore be a deliberate attempt to increase the numbers of senior cavalry officers, perhaps to act as a counterbalance to the infantry and also to increase the pool from which satraps and other senior people were chosen. There were initially 1,800 Companions; reinforcements down to 328 take the total to 3,600, and including the *prodromoi* gives a total of around 4,400. There would have been some losses, however, so a total of 4,000 cavalry in the hipparchies in 328 seems reasonable.

Another theory to explain the reorganization is tactical, in order to make the heavy cavalry more flexible so as to deal with the changing theatre in which Alexander found himself, and the changing character of the fighting that he was conducting. Set-piece battles were no longer being fought or envisaged in the near term, guerrilla warfare was the new norm. If the change was partly tactical then the hipparchies could have taken on an entirely new character, each hipparchy may now have consisted not only of the traditional heavy cavalry, but also of light cavalry. This would have allowed the newly-formed hipparchies to be deployed as skirmishers and quick response troops, but also allowed them to retain their role as front-line combat troops in the more traditional sense. This would have had the overall effect of increasing flexibility within the army and reducing the numbers and the necessity for small individual specialist units.

Yet another theory is that the reorganization was entirely or largely political. There seems to be a significant difference in the distinction and calibre between the eight *ilarchs* named at the Battle of Gaugamela, and the later named hipparchs. Of the former *ilarchs* only three are persons of note: Black Cleitus, who commanded the *agema*; Hegelochus, formerly one of Alexander's admirals; and Demetrius, who retained his position as one of the known hipparchs. The *ilarchs* did have some influence, they were allowed to attend councils of war for example; but they were, with the three exceptions noted above, nonentities.[69] On the other hand, the later hipparchs were some of the most powerful men in the army: Hephaestion, Perdiccas, Craterus, Coenus, White Cleitus and, to a much lesser extent, Demetrius. On this interpretation the change was at least partly due to Alexander's increasing distrust of his principal officers. The sentiments expressed by Black Cleitus before his murder, coming from a previously loyal commander, would have worried Alexander greatly, and he had no way of knowing how far such sentiment went. Thus, dividing the heavy cavalry between as many senior men as possible would dilute any potential risk of an uprising. This does seem very plausible, we know that Alexander made every effort to make himself the focus of the army's loyalty, and it is well documented that he become increasingly paranoid as time went on; but I would argue that at this stage of Alexander's career it was unlikely to have been the primary motivation behind these structural changes. Despite his increasing paranoia, Alexander was always the great tactician and strategist; he was unlikely to put a short term political problem ahead of victory in any of his campaigns. Even though it is unlikely that politics was the primary motivation for the reorganization, it was not necessarily unsound to divide the hipparchies in this way.

This explanation in itself is not a sufficient reason for Alexander to change the whole organization of the cavalry so drastically: he could simply have made these powerful men *ilarchs*, and their status would have automatically increased the status of the rank they occupied. It would seem to be unsound military practice to change or switch well-established names like *lochos* and *ile* (names universal in Greek practice and not only in Macedonia). I think an entirely new name (hipparchy) ought to predispose us to expecting an entirely new thing.[70] It would seem then that the hipparchies were indeed a new creation, and not simply a larger version of an *ile*.

There is a third possibility: that between late 331 and 328 the Companion Cavalry units were gradually reconstructed *exclusively* with the aim of reducing the regional affiliations of each *ile*. After the arrival of Amyntas' reinforcements from Macedonia, new subdivisions of the *ilai* were formed and called *lochoi*. These *lochoi* were then grouped into new units, *tetrarchiai*, perhaps comprising four *lochoi* each from separate *ilai*. The fact that they were from separate *ile* is a key point as this meant that they were from separate areas of Macedonia. There would therefore have been four *tetrarchiai* along with the *agema*. These *tetrarchiai* would then have evolved into the hipparchies that are mentioned from 329 onwards by Ptolemy. If this is true, then the hipparchies were not only larger than the old *ilai* but were also far more heterogeneous, with little or no regional affiliation. This would have the effect of reducing their loyalty to their original regional commanders, who had by then been replaced by the more senior officers mentioned above; it would have the further effect that the troops would feel greater central loyalty to the person of Alexander himself, a key theme noted above. This would be a further indication that Alexander was increasingly distrustful of his unit commanders and wanted to break any loyalty felt by the army for anyone but himself.

I do not believe that these three seemingly competing theories are mutually exclusive. It is certainly true that the hipparchies were larger than the *ilai* (probably 1,000 strong); it also seems likely, judging by their operational activities, that the hipparchies were more versatile than the older units, and therefore may well have comprised some combination of light and heavy cavalry. It also seems likely that Alexander was seeking to increase the status of the Companion Cavalry to act as a balance against the political power of the heavy infantry: several of the hipparchs were former *taxiarchs*; this would no doubt have been presented to them as a promotion, quite rightly so as they were commanding greater numbers with far greater responsibility. It is also likely that Alexander wanted to make the army loyal to him, and not to individual unit commanders who happened to be from the same region as the troops themselves, and of course to reduce the power and influence that men like Parmenio had previously enjoyed. This reorganization seems to have been necessary for several reasons, both military and political, and is an indication of Alexander's vision; that one change to the structure of a section of the army could solve a number of actual or potential problems. We can also conclude that the change was relatively successful, as we seldom hear of the Macedonian cavalry causing Alexander serious political problems; the problems with mutinies late in Alexander's career seem to have stemmed from the infantry, not the cavalry. Their future actions also demonstrate how militarily successful this change was to be.

Orientals

There is no doubt that Alexander made an ever-increasing use of oriental troops after the death of Darius. Arrian tells us of units of Arachosians, Bactrians, Parapamisadae, Scythians, Sogdians and Indians: all were part of the grand army that Alexander assembled by 324.[71] We are also told that the army reached the remarkable, or perhaps unbelievable, size of 120,000 front-line troops at one point (Arrian *Indica* 19.5); this does not take into account the vast numbers of camp followers that would have associated themselves with the host, although Alexander, like Philip before him, made every effort to keep their numbers to a minimum. Only a very small proportion of these could possibly have been Macedonian. This being said, however, it is difficult to ascertain when Alexander first began to employ oriental troops. At the end of 330 Arrian tells us of a new cavalry unit called *hippakontistai*.[72] We know that these troops were something entirely new, because Arrian says as much; we also know that they were mounted javelinmen and were therefore light cavalry, but their ethnic origin is never attested. The theory that they were Persian deserters is highly unlikely given that they also formed a significant part of the garrison of Areia. If they were indeed Persian, this would make them unique in that it was Alexander's general practice to employ mercenaries or allied Greeks as garrison troops, not Persians. They may have been Macedonian or European cavalry: the Paeonians are never again mentioned, and the Paeonians and *hippakontistai* may well be one and the same. The *hippakontistai* were probably Greek light cavalry and would have performed essentially the same role as the *prodromoi*. The key proof was that Arrian links the *hippakontistai* with the regular units of the Macedonian army; the Companions and the Agrianians. This is not to say that they were part of those units, simply that they would have fought alongside them; Alexander was not yet incorporating Persians into the Companion Cavalry units (see below). I think this is more of an indication of Alexander's developing desire to form links between the Macedonians and Persians, as he did with the great marriage ceremony and later with the inclusion of Persian troops into the Macedonian heavy infantry *taxeis* and the ranks of the Companions. This was an extremely important policy: if Alexander was ever to rule the conquered territory, the Persians must come to see him as the rightful successor to the Great Kings, not as a foreign conqueror. This policy was unpopular with the native Macedonians, but Alexander had the vision to realize that if he was to rule the newly-won territory, then he needed the cooperation of the Persian nobility.

The other possible reference to Persian troops employed at an early date is the *hippotoxotai*.[73] There is much less confusion surrounding this unit, with Arrian describing them as Dahae. This particular region surrendered to Alexander in the winter of 328/7 BC and we can only assume that they supplied a contingent shortly after this date. They were most likely horse archers, or perhaps a combination of horse archers and light cavalry, although this is never explicitly stated. The oriental troops that we have mentioned to this point have all been brigaded into specific national units and used either separately or in conjunction with the Companion Cavalry. It remains to be discussed if, and how early, orientals were included in the *hipparchies* alongside the Companions; there are essentially two schools of thought on this.

The first believes that oriental troops had been incorporated within the hipparchies themselves by 324 at the latest, and that the complaints voiced at the Opis mutiny, and its unpopularity amongst the Macedonians, show this quite clearly. Bactrian, Sogdian and Arachosian cavalry, along with horsemen from the Zarangians, Areians, Parthyaeans and the Euacae were all brigaded with the Companion Cavalry.[74] Further to this a fifth hipparchy had been created which was 'not wholly barbarian': this would seem to imply that it would not be unexpected if it *were* wholly barbarian. A more usual description would seem to be 'not wholly Macedonian', suggesting a few Persians. The very fact that Arrian's wording is as it is suggests that the fifth hipparchy was almost entirely Persian. Several oriental nobles had even been included among the ranks of the *agema*; these oriental troops were trained and equipped with Macedonian weapons and not their native javelins. The Zarangians, Areians and Parthyaeans had been incorporated into the army in Carmania in late 325 and the Euacae soon after.[75] The mention of the creation of a fifth hipparchy implies that for some time there had been only four, but we know that in 326 that there had been eight. The reduction from eight to four hipparchies could very well be connected with the losses incurred during the Indian campaign and the march through the Gedrosian Desert: at some point during this time the surviving Companions were consolidated to prevent them from being seriously under strength and operationally ineffective. The increase in strength that must have occurred for the number of hipparchies to be increased from four to five was the result of oriental (and possibly a small number of Macedonian) reinforcements, with the fifth hipparchy consisting of almost entirely oriental troops. I think it is wrong to believe that the fifth hipparchy contained very few oriental troops, and that the fifth hipparchy was originally the *agema*. There is no evidence for this, and Arrian's statement (Arrian 7.6.3) strongly implies that the fifth hipparchy actually consisted mostly of oriental cavalry.

The Opis mutiny passage in Arrian seems to disprove this theory; here the fifth hipparchy and the *agema* are listed as separate entities.[76] On this interpretation of the evidence, orientals were incorporated into the army very late indeed, perhaps 324 or very shortly before this. Given Alexander's need to bring the Persian nobility on board with the new regime in order that he could govern the newly-won territory, it seems impossible to believe that he did not act to make this a reality long before 324. There is also a strong military argument: Alexander needed men, and Persia had an almost limitless supply of good-quality cavalry. It is inconceivable that Alexander would not have made use of them in some way. This would also have had the effect of reducing the numbers of essentially unemployed soldiers in

Persia, with the potential for uprisings, or at least banditry, that that would present.

The second theory is, at least in part, an argument from absence and although it would generally be unwise to make such an argument, here I believe it is the more plausible. It is evident that all of the oriental cavalry that are mentioned in our sources, be they as separate national units or actually incorporated within the hipparchies, represent only a small fraction of those that were potentially available to Alexander. It is also clear that by the end of 330 the central and western satrapies were securely in Alexander's hands but that there is no mention in our sources of any troops from these satrapies having participated in any of Alexander's subsequent campaigns. These were the areas that possessed the finest quality cavalry that the former Persian Empire had to offer, and these were also the people that Alexander needed to win over in order to achieve a measure of security in the new empire.

By contrast, however, troops from the northeast of the former Persian Empire, Bactrians and Sogdians for example, were incorporated by 328, even before those regions were fully 'pacified'. Arrian 7.6.3 (the Opis mutiny grievances passage) certainly refers to the final reorganization of 324; and this, therefore, cannot be used to prove that orientals were in the hipparchies much before this date. The absence of any mention of these western and central Persian troops from our sources is a strong indication that they never served as separate units, but their absence *may* indicate that they were incorporated within the hipparchies from a relatively early date, thus achieving a degree of anonymity.

One of the strongest arguments in favour of this point is its general probability. From 330 there is no doubt that there were very sound military and political reasons to employ troops from the recently conquered central and western satrapies. Militarily, Alexander was always short of quality cavalry; his Macedonians had proven themselves invaluable many times, but they were a limited resource. The nature of the warfare that Alexander was facing after Gaugamela was significantly different from the large set-piece battles that he had fought up to that point, but this did not reduce his need for cavalry, it actually increased it. Troops that could move rapidly in response to any situation would now be at a premium and the Persian Empire was always renowned for its military strength being in its cavalry.

Politically it was also vital to employ Iranian troops. Since Alexander's rejection of Darius' peace overtures in 333 Alexander had gradually been attempting to set himself up as the legitimate alternative to the Great King. I say alternative rather than successor quite deliberately. The old view was that Alexander did indeed portray himself as successor to the Achaemenids, but this is not the case. Alexander in fact used rather different imperial titles and symbolism, and therefore was perhaps more alternative than successor.[77] There could have been no clearer sign of this status after Darius' death than to employ his new subjects in the army. We can also progress a little further along this line and say that politically it would have had the greatest possible impact on the Iranians if they had been included in *ilai*, alongside the Companion Cavalry units, and not simply as separate units as happened with the troops from the northeast of the empire. There is a distinct difference, therefore, between how he employed the oriental cavalry and how he used his allied Greek troops. The Greeks never formed a significant part in the army, they were essentially hostages against the good behaviour of their home city-states. That is to say that they were never incorporated into the Macedonian units in the way the Persians were to become. They were also not used alongside Macedonian units and thus never given that level of responsibility. There are exceptions to this general point; the Agrianians and Thessalians being the most obvious. Their main achievement on the expedition was to supply men for garrisons and new foundations, as well as acting as a second line at Gaugamela and probably at the Granicus and Issus too; here, their role being to prevent the army being encircled. This was, undoubtedly, an important task, but not one that would actually win the battle, although it would help to prevent Alexander being defeated if the battle did not go well. The Persian troops were treated far better by being brigaded within, or at least alongside, the Macedonian units. We hear nothing of the resentment this may have generated amongst the allied Greek contingents, but we can speculate that some resentment would have existed.

There are several passages of Arrian that suggest the hipparchies contained more than exclusively native Macedonian Companion Cavalry, but the evidence is far from conclusive.[78] We must return again to Arrian 7.6.3, the Opis mutiny passage, which may indicate that the main bone of contention amongst the Macedonians was the equipping of Persian troops *already within* the hipparchies with Macedonian cavalry sarissas. If this is indeed a correct interpretation, then the Persian troops were already part of the hipparchies, and they may well have been all through the Indian campaign. Persians could well have been included in the hipparchies from as early as 328. If this is the case then a hipparchy probably would have consisted of one *ile* of Macedonian heavy cavalry and one *ile* of Persian light cavalry - although not all of the Persian troops would have been light cavalry, some would have been more heavily armoured. The central Persian satrapies were strongest in heavy cavalry, these are the type of units that won all of Alexander's set-piece battles, and these are the troops that Alexander would have recruited and utilised if at all possible. A hipparchy, therefore, likely consisted of equal numbers of Macedonians and Persians, each with a greater degree of flexibility than existed before, partly because of the incorporation of the *prodromoi* into the ranks of the Companions as discussed above. The distinction of light and heavy was becoming cloudy as they, together, achieved a greater degree of operational flexibility.

We are still forced to accept, however, the conclusion that until further evidence presents itself, the earliest positive evidence for the inclusion of oriental troops within the hipparchies is 324, or shortly before, even though we can reasonable argue that they were included earlier. We must further accept that we simply do not know why Alexander did not make more effective use of the greatest natural resource of the central satrapies: their cavalry.

Macedonian Cavalry Equipment

In Chapter One the Macedonian infantry sarissa was discussed; it seems appropriate to end this chapter by discussing the possibility of the existence of a specifically-designed cavalry sarissa. Until relatively recent times, historians have tended to fall into one of two camps: either the cavalry did not use a sarissa at all, but something more like the standard spear; or the Macedonian cavalry did use a sarissa of exactly the same dimensions as that employed by the infantry; the possibility that a weapon could have been specifically designed for use by cavalry has been largely ignored, but will be examined here.

The great advantage of the sarissa was that it enabled the wielder to outreach his opponent and be able to strike before his enemy had any chance of landing a blow. This most basic advantage enjoyed by lancers was not specific to the ancient world but has persisted into modern times; the last recorded use of lance-armed cavalry was 3 September 1939 when the Polish Pomorska Cavalry Brigade charged the tanks of the German 3rd Panzer Division, with all-too-predictable results.

We should first examine the ancient and modern literary sources before looking at the pictorial and archaeological evidence for the existence of such a weapon. According to Aristotle, Alexander's cavalry used a sword as well as the sarissa; we also know that the anonymous Byzantine historian contrasts the infantry's 'long spear' with the 'spear' of the cavalry.[79] Appian, on the other hand, uses similar language for the infantry weapon to that of the cavalry. Arrian also tells us that when Alexander enrolled Persians into his army he replaced the Persian javelin with the cavalry spear, ie the sarissa. Aelian gives us the vital information that the cavalry sarissa was no shorter than 8 cubits in length. The terms 'sarissa' or 'cavalry sarissa' are the ones that I will try to maintain throughout this section, although I will also use 'lance' at times. The ancient sources seem to use a range of confusing terminology to refer to what is probably the same thing, the cavalry sarissa. We see sarissa, pike, *dory*, lance, *xyston*, spear and *kontos*, all seemingly interchangeable. Strabo gives us a good indication as to the weight of the cavalry sarissa when he tells us that it could be used both in hand-to-hand combat and that it could be thrown like a javelin, something which was quite simply impossible to do with the infantry sarissa. Asclepiodotus also affirms that the cavalry use something different from other cavalry of the day, stating: 'The cavalry which fights at close quarters uses...long spears and is therefore called *doratophoroi*, or also *xystophoroi*'.[80] There are also Arrian's numerous references to *sarissophoroi*. As mentioned earlier, these were the *prodromoi*, who, in certain circumstances, were equipped with the cavalry sarissa during the set-piece battles. This again illustrates that Alexander's Macedonian cavalry occasionally used something other than the traditional javelin.[81]

From the literary sources we also know that the shaft of the sarissa was made of cornel wood; this had been used for javelins since at least the seventh century partly because of its superior combination of elasticity and strength, but also for its relatively low impact resistance; it would break rather than unseating the cavalryman from his horse when the user made contact with the enemy.

The cavalry sarissa had two spear points, one affixed to each end of the shaft. This was necessary because if the spear broke the cavalryman could simply turn the weapon around and use the other end.[82] In this regard the cavalry sarissa can be contrasted with that of the infantry which had only one spear point; on the rear of that weapon was a butt-spike which could be driven into the ground so as to impale an onrushing cavalryman, or indeed an infantryman.

From the surviving literary evidence alone, considering nothing else, we can conclude that the cavalry sarissa was:

- 8 cubits long.
- made from cornel wood.
- equipped with a spear point at both ends of the shaft.
- light enough to be thrown like a javelin.

Visual evidence for ancient weapons is often problematic, sometimes due to the substrate upon which the image is placed, its degree of preservation, or indeed the size of the image in the case of coins: but there is perhaps evidence to support the literary sources. A funerary bas-relief from Apollonia in Epirus shows a mounted figure holding a double-pointed cavalry sarissa. The aft point of the weapon can clearly be seen to be larger than the fore point, presumably to add weight to the rear of the weapon so it could be held closer to the rear, allowing more of the spear to protrude in front of the cavalryman. It is impossible to determine the length of the weapon because of the size of the funerary monument; the artist found it necessary to foreshorten the spear in order for it to fit within the parameters of the sculpture.

The fresco from the Naoussa tomb depicting a Macedonian cavalryman drilling with his groom shows the sarissa being held in the 3:5 position; that is to say forty per cent of the lance protruding to the rear of the cavalryman and the other sixty per cent to the front. This, therefore, confirms that the aft point must have been heavier than the fore point allowing the weapon to be balanced at the 3:5 position. Some have argued that there was no significant difference between the sarissa used by the cavalry and that used by the infantry, and furthermore that there was no difference in size or weight between the spear point at each end of the shaft of the cavalry sarissa.[83] This must be wrong for it to have been balanced as it clearly is in the visual depictions we have examined; there is further archaeological evidence for this point too.

The Alexander Mosaic, now in the Naples museum, depicts the presence of a strap on the lance which the cavalryman would use to prevent the weapon slipping in his hand; it would also be used to ensure the weapon could not be easily dropped, as the loop of the strap would be wound round the wrist. The strap would also be used to carry the weapon over the shoulder whilst the trooper marching, to prevent any accidental injuries to those both in front and behind him. In the foreground of the mosaic, beneath Alexander, is a discarded lance. The lance is discarded presumably because both of its spear points are missing, but the strap and wrist-loop are still present. Behind Alexander and to the left there is a Boeotian-helmeted figure that is striking an overhead blow with the aft point of his broken sarissa. These two figures, the Boeotian-helmeted figure and that of Alexander, depict the two basic combat strokes allowed by the cavalry sarissa.

We can therefore conclude several points from the pictorial evidence:

• the cavalry sarissa had weapon points at both ends of the shaft.
• the shaft is of approximately uniform diameter along its length and when used in combat is held in the 3:5 position.
• it is held in one hand and can be used either to thrust underarm or to stab down on an enemy using an over-arm stroke.
• the cavalry sarissa includes a strap for both carrying the lance over the shoulder whilst marching, and to help the rider grip and hold on to the lance during combat.

The number of sarissa heads, hoplite spearheads and javelin heads that have been found are of a sufficient quantity and quality to be able to clearly distinguish between them. The hoplite spear found at Vergina in Tumulus LXVIII, Burial E, had an iron spearhead of 27.5cm and weighed 127g, as well as an iron butt-spike of 6.35cm and weighing 42.5g; there were also fragments of wood found in between the two, strongly suggesting that they once belonged to the same weapon. The infantry sarissa was considerably larger, the iron head being 51cm long and weighing 1.224kg, and the iron butt-spike measuring 45.75cm and weighing 1.046kg.[84] The cavalry sarissa, on the other hand, lies somewhere between the two; its aft spearpoint consisted of a double-edged flaring blade 49.5cm long, weighing 526g. The fore head had a similarly double-edged flaring blade, but was rather smaller at 28cm long, weighing 267g. The two spearheads of the cavalry sarissa can be identified as coming from the same weapon, aside from being found together, thus:

• the presence of two spear points of such dissimilar size supports the visual evidence.
• the two spear heads have identical socket diameters.

• the identical method of affixing the heads to the shaft: both spear heads are pierced by two diametrically opposed holes through which nails could be driven.

• the socket dimensions are similar to some other identified spear points, but the large double-edged flaring nature of the lance heads sets them apart from other spear points.

• the smaller socket diameter and lighter weight of the cavalry sarissa as against the infantry weapon, clearly differentiate the two types of weapon.

A review of the available evidence allows us to make several general conclusions: first of all, that the cavalry sarissa did in fact exist; and second that it was of a different design and construction from that used by the infantry. The cavalry sarissa was around 2.75m long and weighed 1.9kg, thus confirming Strabo's claim that it was light enough to be thrown. The lance itself had two spearheads, one considerably larger than the other, the larger of the two being at the rear, partially to act as a counter weight, allowing the weapon to be held in the 3:5 position. The weapon was also fitted with a strap to allow the user greater flexibility and to reduce the risk of the lance being dropped in combat.[85]

Chapter 4

Allied Cavalry

—⚬—

Thessalian Cavalry

Probably the most important non–Macedonian contingent within the whole army during the early stages of the war was the Thessalian cavalry. The Thessalian contingent was not newly recruited by Alexander, but had fought alongside the Macedonians under Philip for some years before his death. They had, for instance, gained distinction during the Battle of Chaeronea, where they may have taken part in the final cavalry charge led by the young Alexander, although the details of this battle are sketchy at best. They evidently performed admirably, as it was Alexander who defeated the Theban Sacred Band.

At the outset of the expedition Alexander commanded 1,800 Companion Cavalry, and it seems that he had a similar number of Thessalians. It is not certain if he left any Thessalian cavalry with his regent, Antipater, in Greece. I would argue not, however, given that it would not have been terribly difficult to raise more from Thessaly as they were required. Keeping a standing force would not be necessary; he had enough Macedonian troops to keep Greece in order, or so it appeared before the revolt of Agis. These troops had been raised from among the nobility of Thessaly, which had a long-standing reputation for producing the finest cavalry in the Greek world. The initial 1,800 men were supplemented by a group of 200 reinforcements that reached the army at Gordium in 334. These troops were among the first batch of reinforcements received by Alexander. Arrian mentions no others during the early stages of the campaign, although it is possible that there were some that we simply do not hear about; this would be understandable as the sources had more interesting events to narrate throughout most of the campaign rather than the arrival of reinforcements. It seems plausible enough that there was a wave of reinforcements arriving with the army throughout 333, but there is no positive evidence for this at all in the sources. It should be stated, however, that it is unlikely that any more Thessalians arrived during the early stages of the campaign and that their nominal strength probably never exceeded 2,000. We can assume this because the number of known units does not significantly change in the early stages of the campaign.

It is unclear from our sources what Alexander did with these 200 reinforcements at Gordium. It could be that they were incorporated amongst existing *ilai* to make up for losses incurred up to that point, but I believe this would be based upon the false assumption that the Thessalians had sustained losses of around 200 men already, and this seems not to have been the case. I would argue, however, that the reinforcements were indeed incorporated into existing *ilai*, but this would have led to an increase in unit strength, and not act as replacements for losses. In the early stages of the campaign the Thessalians were not heavily involved in the fighting and so their losses would have been minimal and certainly not ten per cent of their nominal strength: the only major action they saw was at the Battle of the Granicus River, and a ten per cent loss here is unrealistic. The only other option would be to assume that a ninth *ile* was created, but our sources do not even hint at this; so we are left to assume that the existing *ilai* were strengthened and the existing eight *ilai* were maintained. Losses on campaign would have reduced them back to their nominal 200 over time.

We are not told explicitly how the Thessalians were organized, but it would seem logical if it were along the same lines as for the Macedonian Companion Cavalry. That is to say, they were organized into eight *ilai* of 200 men; one of which was probably double strength, the so-called Pharsalian *ile*. The Pharsalian *ile* would have performed the same role as the royal squadron of the Companions; they would have been effectively the bodyguard of their commander in battle.[86] This double strength *ile* is the only one Arrian, or any of our sources, explicitly names; but the others were no doubt also named after prominent Thessalian cities or regions, again echoing the Companion Cavalry.

At the outset of the campaign, up to the Battle of the Granicus, the Thessalians were under the command of Calas, a man who had served under Parmenio on the expeditionary force and was surely one of 'Parmenio's men'. Alexander removed him from this position immediately after the battle, however, appointing him satrap of Hellespontine Phrygia.

Alexander then appointed Philip, son of Menelaus, as Calas' successor. Parmenio of course had overall command of these troops during the set-piece battles, and indeed at other times. They acted as his personal bodyguard in the same way as the Companions did with Alexander. There are a number of ways to view the treatment of Calas; it is certainly true that Alexander took every effort to remove men from positions within the army that were not of his choosing. These people are frequently referred to as either Philip's or Parmenio's men. Calas' removal could be part of such a grand strategy, one which in actuality took several years to complete, perhaps only ending with the murder of Philotas and Parmenio. Calas' experience of this region as part of the expeditionary force made him an ideal candidate, and the only logical choice, to occupy a governorship in that area. We can further argue that, given that the satrapy of Paphlagonia was also added to Calas' territory, he could not have been seen as anything other than a loyal officer. Having said this, however, Alexander was no doubt happy to have replaced him within the army with one of his own men, thus reducing the power base of Parmenio slightly.

The Thessalian cavalry carried virtually the same equipment as the Companions, but one superficial distinction can be made. The two horsemen depicted on the Alexander sarcophagus, one hunting, the other in battle, wear the distinctive Thessalian cloak and can probably therefore be identified with this contingent. The cloak is identified by the two points that hang down both in front of and behind the figures. Other than the cloak, there seems very little to distinguish them from the Companions in terms of dress or equipment. We can only assume that the Thessalians previously used the javelin but were now equipped and trained in the use of the cavalry sarissa, as were the Companion Cavalry.

It is frequently argued that the Thessalians 'performed much the same functions as the Companions', but this is demonstrably not the case.[87] They did form the bodyguard for Parmenio in the same way that the Companions did to Alexander, but their actual role in the set-piece battles was significantly different. The Companions were the main offensive weapon of the army, trained and employed to punch a hole in the enemy's line, drive troops through and then to wheel on the enemy centre. An attack of this nature, if correctly coordinated, would ensure that the enemy centre would be attacked from two directions at the same time, both from the side by the cavalry and from the front by the advancing heavy infantry. This strategy is essentially Alexander's hallmark and is an eerie foreshadowing of the

German *Blitzkrieg* strategy developed, in the main, by Heinz Guderian. The Thessalians on the other hand were assigned to fight defensive actions on the left wing, to prevent the army from being outflanked or encircled by superior Persian numbers. This is certainly the case during at least the battles of Issus and Gaugamela, although their role at the Granicus is unclear. This can clearly be seen at Issus, for example: Alexander attacked across the Pinarus River on the right, with Parmenio holding the line between the heavy infantry and the sea on the left to prevent the army from being outflanked. Their role was perhaps equally important as that performed by the Companions on the right but was certainly not the same.

Although the Thessalians were without question amongst the finest troops in the Macedonian order of battle, Alexander evidently saw them as being far from indispensable. In 331, whilst at Ecbatana, Alexander disbanded the Thessalian cavalry and all other allied contingents, ordering them back to the Aegean. A very generous settlement was given and an escort was organized to take them back to the Aegean coast. It seems that the Thessalians were marching on foot with a cavalry escort, having evidently sold their horses, presumably to the Companions. Attrition amongst horses on the expedition must have been particularly high. Any who wished were allowed to re-enrol with the army, but their status would no longer be that of allies, but of mercenaries. Each man who remained with the army was given a massive bonus of three talents; many evidently stayed. The distinction between mercenaries and allies is perhaps a fine one; they would most likely receive the same rate of pay as they had done previously, and would be equipped and probably organized in the same manner, but Alexander's willingness to risk losing them all by disbanding them shows that he felt they were not critical to his future success. It could also be an indication of increasing use of oriental cavalry; the cavalry from the central satrapies were of similar quality and potentially available in far greater numbers than a mere 2,000.

Why though, were the allied troops disbanded at this point? Diodorus perhaps gives us the answer. While at Ecbatana, Diodorus tells us that Alexander 'was aware that the Macedonians regarded Darius' death as the end of the campaign'.[88] If Diodorus is right that even the Macedonians felt this way, then it is almost certain that the Greek allies did. Beside this point, the Greeks had been obliged to aid Alexander in the destruction of the Persian Empire; the death of Darius signalled that this goal had been achieved and thus the obligation of the city-states was fulfilled; essentially the war of the League of Corinth was at an end. Many of them chose to stay, no doubt for the financial incentives offered by Alexander, but, as noted above, they were now employed as mercenaries.

There were purely military reasons for the disbanding of the Thessalians too; Alexander would have been aware that the terrain he was about to enter in the north-east of the former Persian Empire would not lend itself to the kind of set-piece battles that had given him victory over Darius in the previous few years. There would, therefore, be no need for a primarily defensive detachment of cavalry; the main fighting would be done by the Companions and the Macedonian heavy infantry units, along with the appropriate light infantry. Those allied troops that re-enlisted were finally and fully disbanded less than a year later, thus supporting Alexander's evident belief that they were no longer necessary to the overall success of the campaign.

Other Allied Cavalry

The Greek states of the League of Corinth were obliged to provide cavalry as well as infantry to the army of invasion. Not all states were required or expected to furnish cavalry; what was required of each would have depended to an extent on what they were best able to provide. A precedent existed to this policy in the form of the old Delian League; many states chose to contribute money rather than ships, which had made Athens' position even stronger. Diodorus tells us that 600 Greek cavalry commanded by Erigyius crossed the Hellespont with the main body of the army in 334 BC. These 600 can probably be equated with the three *ilai* of allied horse at Gaugamela.[89] These three squadrons were from the Peloponnese and Achaea, from Phthiotis and Malis, and from Locris and Phocis. These troops seem to have been stationed on the right wing. As a complement to the allied cavalry on the right, there was also a contingent stationed on the left wing at Gaugamela. This second group were commanded by Coeranus and probably numbered 600, also divided into three *ilai*, as with those on the right. This group may well have contained the Boeotians (mentioned below), the Acarnanians and the Aetolians, along with perhaps the Eleians. No individual state initially seems to have made a contribution of a full *ile*; rather troops from different states in the same geographical area were brigaded together.

These cavalry were important to Alexander's set-piece battles, and played a significant role in his victories. One of Alexander's hallmark strategies was always to draw the enemy onto terrain of his choosing. This could be on a grand scale by enticing the Persians into the narrows at Issus, or on a much smaller scale by drawing enemy units out of formation during a battle. At both the Granicus and Gaugamela, Alexander began the attack by essentially sacrificing a body of allied horse. He ordered a small unit of allied cavalry to attack the enemy left, drawing forward a much larger and stronger body of Persian cavalry. The attack never went well, but it succeeded in drawing the Persians out so they were in a vulnerable position for the Companion Cavalry to fall upon them whilst they were in disarray. On the face of it this shows a callous disregard for the allied Greek cavalry, but the tactic always resulted in victory.

We often do not have a complete picture of what the allied cavalry units were doing at any given time. For example, when Alexander entered Egypt it appears that only a part of the army accompanied him; specifically, the Macedonian troops along with the Agrianians. Whilst Alexander was in Egypt our sources dwell upon Alexander's activities and almost totally ignore the rest of the army. We do know that the allied cavalry had been attached to the satrap of Syria temporarily, after the Battle of Issus. We can perhaps assume that at some point a batch of allied cavalry reinforcements arrived from Greece. Curtius reports a conversation between Darius and the exiled Charidemus in which Charidemus mentions an otherwise unknown contingent of Acarnanians and Aetolians.[90] The speech is almost certainly apocryphal, as Charidemus was exiled from Athens some time before, at the orders of Alexander. Curtius, in creating this conversation, could well be using sources that were aware of the existence of these two contingents. If they are genuine then they must have been part of a batch of reinforcements of which we otherwise hear nothing. We also know that a contingent from Boeotia reached the army in Asia at some point: an inscription found at Orchomenus records a dedication made by those who served with Alexander, also mentioning their *ilarch*.

Balkan Cavalry

As mentioned in the previous chapter the army also contained a contingent of 300 Paeonian *prodromoi*. These troops were probably supplied from two areas; one was Paeonia and the other Odrysia. The Paeonians were commanded by Ariston, a member of the royal house of Paeonia. The Odrysians on the other hand were commanded by Agathon, a Macedonian.

We can assume that these *prodromoi* were equipped in a similar way to the Macedonian *prodromoi*, as discussed in the previous chapter, but their national dress was significantly different. They were dressed in long-sleeved tunics and wore a crested helmet and may have used a panther-skin saddlecloth. These troops are those mentioned as being with the army at the crossing of the Hellespont, described by Diodorus as part of the '900 Thracian and Paeonian *prodromoi*'.

Chapter 5

Other Mercenaries and Allies

—◦◦◦—

A distinction between mercenaries and allied troops certainly existed within the Macedonian order of battle; we saw this with the Thessalian cavalry in the previous chapter for example. The distinction drawn by Alexander was not sharp, however, and could lead to some confusion. We must first therefore clarify what these terms actually mean before we consider the individual contingents themselves.

The meaning of the term 'mercenary' would seem at first sight obvious: a soldier who fights for pay. But of course everyone in Alexander's army was being paid, including the Macedonian and allied contingents. I believe that we can narrow the meaning down to 'someone who fights without a political imperative', that is a soldier who is not compelled to fight by his city-state, but does so purely for personal reasons. The distinction therefore becomes a little clearer, but the status of the Balkan troops in the army is still problematic. They are one of the contingents whose status changed whilst on campaign; the Balkan troops came from peoples who were more or less formally subject to the king of Macedonia, so that it is difficult to make the distinction between whether they were mercenaries or allies. It is perhaps best to avoid a splitting of hairs and to call them all mercenaries, because if they were allies in the first place they certainly became mercenaries later. I will here consider them amongst the allied contingent, as they were initially of that status, and Diodorus certainly does not include them amongst the mercenaries in his troop list of 334 BC.[91]

By the time of the accession of Alexander in Macedonia, mercenary soldiers formed an integral part, not just of the Macedonian army, but also that of Persia and a number of the Greek city-states. The mercenary soldier himself, however, had undergone considerable change. In the fifth century, mercenaries were few in number and employment opportunities were limited. Their first large scale employment in Greece was during the

Peloponnesian War, and was at first confined to the Spartan side, Athens having no access to the large recruiting grounds of Arcadia. It is also the case that Pericles' defensive strategy had little need of mercenaries. Athens' first recorded use of hoplite mercenaries was on the Sicilian expedition, and even here there were only 250 'Mantineans and other mercenary troops'.[92] Persia tended not to employ Greek mercenaries in large numbers in the fifth century, the first large scale employment being Cyrus' force of 10,000 so brilliantly described by Xenophon. Mercenaries in the fifth century tended to be grouped into one of the following classifications:

- Archers, often from Crete - Archery, throughout all periods of history, was a specialized field and required considerable training. It was very difficult for a citizen hoplite to acquire the necessary skills and so specialists were hired. Crete is often mentioned as a source of such troops throughout the fifth and fourth centuries, and it even furnished a contingent in Alexander's army; although Alexander also employed a native Macedonian contingent of archers.
- Cavalry - Usually few in number, primarily because of the expense involved, and because the geography of Greece also generally did not lend itself well to cavalry engagements, with a few notable topographical exceptions.
- Hoplites - Troops armed and equipped in the same manner as a citizen soldier; a heavily armed infantryman wearing a breastplate and often greaves, and carrying a spear. Their main offensive weapon was weight of numbers, hoplite battles could perhaps be thought of as a giant rugby scrum. Heavily-armed hoplites were the main fighting force on either side in the fifth and into the fourth century.
- Peltasts - Light-armed troops carrying a small shield and little or no body armour. Their effectiveness was based almost entirely on their mobility. Most mercenaries in the fourth century fell into this group after the 'reforms of Iphicrates' early in that century.

Iphicrates' Reforms

Iphicrates was born towards the end of the fifth century into a poor and rather obscure Athenian family. Despite his lowly background he rose to a position of command in Athens, fighting in a number of campaigns including the Corinthian War and the Social War, he also spent time in Persian service after the Peace of Antalcidas. Diodorus places his peltast reforms after 374, following his Persian sojourn, using his experiences prior to that date to develop this new type of soldier.[93] The exact dating of the reforms is not relevant here, but their nature certainly is, as it was this type of soldier that constituted the bulk of Alexander's mercenary forces. I have also tried to argue earlier that Alexander's heavy infantry were essentially a version of Iphicratean peltasts, being equipped as they were with a small shield and very little body armour.

The primary sources of information that we have for the peltast reforms of Iphicrates are Diodorus and Nepos, both of whose accounts are very similar. According to them the most significant changes were as follows:[94]

> Iphicrates replaced the large (shield) of the Greeks by the light *pelte*, which had the advantage that it protected the body while allowing the wearer more freedom of movement; the soldiers who had formerly carried the [large hoplite shield] and who were called hoplites, were henceforth called peltasts after the name of their new shields; their new spears were half as long again or even twice as long as the old ones, the new swords were also double in length, In addition Iphicrates introduced light and easily untied footwear, and the bronze harness was replaced by a linen covering, which although it was lighter, still protected the body.

Diodorus regards these changes as having been introduced into the existing hoplite troops and in the process discounts the possibility of already existing peltast-style light infantry. Diodorus' failure to realize the existence of peltast troops before Iphicrates is indeed very striking. In this omission Diodorus shows his serious lack of understanding of the military situation of the day. Modern commentators have frequently been struck with the absurdity of this, and have taken up an opposite attitude. For them the change was a trivial one and consisted chiefly in the standardizing of the existing, but rather haphazard, peltast equipment. This argument, however, simply will not do. It assumes that the light-armed skirmishers of earlier narratives were equipped in the same manner that Diodorus describes. This simply cannot be the case; light-armed skirmishers would not have carried a sword and spear twice the length of those carried by hoplites. Earlier narratives also tell of peltasts actually throwing their spears. If Iphicrates was standardizing that which already existed then why did he not provide his troops with these throwing spears? We are surely not to believe that they carried these as well. Some other explanation must be sought.

Was Iphicrates actually inventing a new type of peltast, one with specific and specialized equipment? The other extreme view is that Iphicratean peltasts were in no way different from Thracian peltasts. On this interpretation, Iphicrates' reforms were of little significance, as troops of exactly the same type existed already in Thrace. The truth probably lies somewhere between these two extreme positions. There was probably no uniformity of peltast equipment before Iphicrates, some using primarily throwing spears, some longer spears, still others using swords of various sizes. The size of the shield probably varied too. I suspect therefore that Iphicrates studied the light infantry of his day and based his reforms around choosing from the various groups the equipment that best suited the type of soldier that he was trying to create. We may see Iphicrates therefore not as creating something entirely new, or as standardizing that which already existed, but as refining the equipment and tactics of the peltasts of his day.

Mercenaries had not been a significant part of the military forces of the city-states in the fifth century. There was, on the one hand, very little fiscal means to support such troops, and, on the other, a generally held belief that it was a citizen's duty to take up arms and defend his *polis* as need arose. Any Greek mercenaries that did exist were generally employed in Persia or Egypt. Mercenaries were also employed in Sicily in significant numbers from an early date. By 481 it seems possible that Gelon, tyrant of Syracuse, maintained an army that included as many as 15,000 mercenaries. They presumably constituted a significant part of the army that won the decisive victory over the Carthaginians at Himera. The most significant event that sparked a major increase in the employment of mercenary troops on mainland Greece was the Peloponnesian War. The Peloponnesian states were the first to employ mercenaries in great numbers. These mercenaries were initially not light-armed troops but hoplites from Arcadia. Athens was slow to hire such troops, largely because of the geographical difficulty in reaching them, but by the end of the war mercenaries of all kinds were finding employment on both sides. The reasons for this change lay in the nature of the war itself. The war was prolonged and almost continuous and there were few large-scale set piece battles fought; most engagements were on a small scale and fought by troops who were relatively lightly equipped and very mobile. Mercenaries were simply better at this kind of combat than heavily armoured hoplites. The hiring of mercenaries was made possible now, and less so earlier, by the relative prosperity of the warring states as compared to earlier in the fifth century.

The end of the Peloponnesian War did not see an ending of the employment of mercenaries in Greece. The peace itself led to a large number of men who had become accustomed to earning their living as hired soldiers suddenly becoming unemployed. This would generally have a destabilizing effect upon any society, but they would not have stayed unemployed for long. The political situation in Greece in the fourth century meant that there were always potential paymasters. Their other great sphere of employment, Persia, was also undergoing change. The central authority of the Persian Empire had begun to weaken. The local governors and satraps grew more independent and ambitious. Their position needed military support, and they found it most readily in Greek mercenaries. It had long been recognized that mercenaries formed a more secure power base for tyrants, rather than citizen soldiers whose loyalty was more open to question if a usurper came along. Greek mercenary infantry in Persian service continually proved themselves more capable than anything that the native Persians were able to achieve, so the great king himself was also forced to hire his own contingents to keep pace with his potentially disloyal satraps. We see this to be true during the reign of Alexander too: the only quality infantry that Darius had at his disposal were the Greek mercenaries. Initially 20,000 strong at the Granicus, they had been reduced to perhaps only 2,000 by the time of Gaugamela. This was because of successive losses at the Granicus and Issus, but probably due to desertion too as it became apparent that Alexander was a more attractive paymaster. The League of Corinth had specifically outlawed a Greek taking up arms against another Greek; this decree had meant little at the outset of the campaign when Persia looked like a good bet for victory. At the time of the battle of Gaugamela in 331, however, Darius found it almost impossible to hire more Greek hoplite mercenaries. This was partly because he was no longer an attractive employer, partly because of the distance from Greece, and partly because Alexander was hiring them in increasing numbers, thus reducing the available pool.

Philip

The use of mercenary troops became commonplace in the fourth century, spreading ultimately to Macedonia. Our sources give us very little information about the composition or effectiveness of the Macedonian army at the accession of Philip, save to imply that it was strong in cavalry and very weak in infantry. Mercenaries had been used in Macedonia before the reign of Philip, and had perhaps even been employed by Philip himself before he became king. Carystius of Pergamon relates the following:[95]

> Speusippus, on hearing that Philip was speaking ill of Plato, wrote in a letter somewhat as follows: People do not know that Philip actually secured the beginnings of his kingship through Plato. For Plato sent Euphraeus of Oreus to Perdiccas, who persuaded him to allot a portion of land to Philip. From that revenue he kept a standing army, and so when Perdiccas died, with his army ready he threw himself into political power.

The story does not come to us directly and is unlikely to be completely accurate; it may, however, contain some degree of truth.

In order to hire any significant number of mercenaries, vast quantities of gold and silver were required. Throughout the fourth century the city-states struggled financially to cope with the almost continuous warfare that they were presented with: Macedonia, however, was in a very different position. After 357, with the capture of Amphipolis, Philip had access to the gold, and perhaps more importantly, the silver mines of Mount Pangaeus. These mines were then worked with more energy than they ever had been before, to such an extent that they produced 1,000 talents a year for the treasuries of Macedonia. This is probably about the same as Athens had produced from her empire, although Athens peaked at 1,460 talents in 425; although we should note that some states provided ships instead of money. As the Athenian Empire grew, however, the numbers of member states who made their contributions in kind declined. Athens preferred to receive financial contributions as this made her position more secure, all of the fleet being provided by her and therefore loyal to her alone. The new income ensured that Philip need never be short of mercenaries, but to what extent did he actually employ them? The first recorded instance of the employment of mercenaries in Philip's army came in 352 when they aided in the capture of Pharcedon in Thessaly; although they may well have been present the previous year when Philip was defeated by Onomarchus.[96] It was also at this same period that Chares the Athenian general hosted a feast in the agora to celebrate a victory over the mercenaries of Philip. Mercenaries were certainly present in the army of occupation in Phocis in 346 at the end of the Sacred War, and they appear several times in later years – as reinforcements to Messene and Argos in 344, as well as at Megara. Four mercenary armies are also known on Euboea, and more are known in the Chersonese, and probably at Chaeronea in 338.

Diodorus' account of the career of Philip is lacking in details. In fact it is almost totally devoid of any detail after 346 BC, and thus it is very difficult indeed to make any kind of assessment as to how important mercenaries were in the Macedonia that Philip created. Diodorus' account of the Battle of Chaeronea is a good example of this; he gives no details on the armies themselves and almost suggests that the victory was due entirely to the bravery and heroism of the young Alexander. Demosthenes, on the surface, gives us a little more information. He lays great stress upon Philip's reliance upon mercenaries, even to the extent of belittling the heavy infantry:[97]

> and you hear of Philip going wherever he wants, not by virtue of commanding a phalanx of hoplites, but because he has fitted out light-armed infantry, horsemen, archers, mercenaries and that sort of army.

He also emphasizes Philip's great wealth, implying that it was this that enabled him to buy 'this sort of army', and therefore essentially to buy success rather than earning it with a more traditional army of hoplites. Demosthenes, however, was writing for an Athenian audience and with a very specific agenda; he said whatever it suited him to say and what his audience wished to hear. Demosthenes, therefore, only really tells us that Philip employed mercenaries to some extent, which we already knew. The only other thing that he tells us is that Philip probably made greater use of mercenaries than was usual at the time, but tells us nothing about tactics or numbers.

The use of mercenaries by Philip can be divided into two distinct periods, separated by the year 346. Before this date only three mentions are made of mercenaries in the Macedonian army: the first against Chares, and the second in the capture of Pharcedon in 353-2. The third instance was when he loaned a contingent of mercenaries to Phocion in 348. During the early part of Philip's reign his Macedonian national army was in the process of being trained, and I believe it likely that mercenaries played a far greater role in military operations during this period than these sparse references would seem to indicate. After 346, when Philip had gained control of much of Greece, mercenaries were used to form garrisons at strategic points throughout the Greek world; this was a policy that Alexander continued and greatly expanded upon, as we shall see. They also continued to be used in a combat role as evidenced by the composition of the expeditionary force sent to Asia Minor by Philip in 336.

Alexander

The majority of mercenaries employed by Alexander at the beginning of his reign would have accompanied Alexander into Asia, or were already there, having been sent by Philip with the expeditionary force in 336. It is unlikely that any would have been left behind with the standing army in Macedonia; this would have been an unnecessary expense. At the outset of the campaign, funds were at a premium; we know that Alexander left himself with a huge amount of personal debt before 334, relying upon the conquest of Persia to restore Macedonia's fortunes. Having said this, Alexander had left garrisons at strategic points throughout Greece.[98] These garrisons would almost certainly have been mercenaries; this being the beginning of a trend that Alexander used throughout his career.

In his detailed order of battle for 334, Diodorus tells us that of the 32,000 infantry in the army of invasion, 5,000 were mercenaries, although this figure assumes that the Balkan troops were allied rather than mercenaries. 5,000 seems to be a remarkably small number as a percentage of the total, only 15.6 per cent. There are four main reasons for this:[99]

- Mercenaries, historically, had not constituted a large part of Greek armies.
- Philip seems to have seriously depleted the Macedonian treasury, leaving Alexander with very little money with which to hire mercenaries.
- In 334, Darius was a competing paymaster. The Persians had

always been a large employer of Greek mercenaries and had the resources to hire as many as they required at any given time. Darius was also a seemingly attractive prospective employer as the Persian Empire was vast in comparison to Macedonia.

• Alexander had very little need for mercenaries in his army at the outset of the campaign.

It has long been realized, however, that Diodorus' figure of 5,000 mercenaries carries with it some serious problems. During the first year of the campaign in Asia, up to the Battle of Issus, Alexander left behind garrisons at Side, Mytilene, and possibly Ephesus and Miletus too. A force of 3,000 mercenary infantry was also left to complete the reduction of Halicarnassus after Alexander advanced further into Asia, and to act as a garrison for the satrapy of Caria. Our sources do not tell us the size of the garrisons left in Side and Mytilene, or the numbers of casualties in combat to this point, although Alexander did not use mercenaries as front line troops and so their casualty figures were probably small. But we can perhaps safely assume that the total left behind before Issus would amount to in excess of 5,000, more than the number with which Alexander had invaded Asia. To the best of our knowledge the only additional mercenaries that Alexander received were the 300 that defected to Alexander from the Persian garrison at Miletus.

The problem arises when we look at the battle of Issus. There clearly seems to be two bodies of mercenaries that, I believe, formed a reserve line behind the Macedonian heavy infantry. Arrian's description of the dispositions of Alexander's army is not as detailed as we would like; he does not tell us, for example, the number of mercenaries present. It is probable that such a force, forming a second line, would have been fairly considerable; between 5,000 and 8,000 is not an unreasonable estimate. If we take the lower of these two figures, this leaves us with a significant shortfall. There are only two possible explanations: either we make up the deficit by suggesting that these troops were the remnants of the expeditionary force, about whose fate we otherwise know nothing, or there was a draft of reinforcements from Greece between 334 and 333 upon which our sources are silent. It would seem that the former explanation is the more plausible, as it is unsafe to invent troops just for our own convenience and to fill a gap in our available evidence.

Soon after landing in Asia, then, Alexander seems to have been in the following position with regard to his mercenaries:

5,000	Army of Invasion	Diodorus, 17.17.3.
-2,500	Garrison at Ephesus	Bosworth, 1980, 134.
-3000	Garrison of Caria	Arrian, 1.23.6.
-2000	Garrisons at Side, Mytilene, Miletus? and Estimated Casualties	Arrian, 1.23.6.
+300	Miletus	Arrian, 1.19.6.

Assuming that there were around 5,000 at Issus, enough to form the presumed second line there (I am assuming that there was indeed a second defensive line at Issus, much as at Gaugamela), this therefore leaves around 7,200 mercenaries unaccounted for. These must be the remnants of the 10,000 sent to Asia as an expeditionary force in 336. This does raise the question as to how Philip could have afforded so many mercenaries at this time; all we can say is that his financial reserves must have been, to say the least, stretched, because it seems undeniable that these missing troops were mercenaries.

Logic may tend to suggest that with every successful campaign of Alexander, more and more mercenaries would flock to his banner: a successful general is always a far more attractive paymaster than an unsuccessful one. For example, Darius had 20,000 Greek mercenary hoplites at the Granicus in 334, and only around 2,000 at Gaugamela three years later. He did not lack for money even then, but still found Greek mercenaries impossible to acquire. We also need to note that after Issus Alexander was not short of funds and thus also in a position to employ mercenaries easily. This does not seem to have been the case, however, at least until that pivotal year of 331. Our sources only record two batches of mercenary reinforcements received by Alexander before Gaugamela: 4,000 from Sidon and 3,000 from Chios. We are also told of a mercenary garrison of 4,000 left behind in Egypt; these must be the reinforcements from Sidon, as they are not mentioned at the Battle of Gaugamela. Although the total number of mercenary troops may have increased slightly during the first three years of the campaign, so did the number of Macedonian troops and therefore the proportion of mercenaries to Macedonians remained almost constant. Reinforcements were arriving at roughly the same rate as they were required to form garrisons in the newly-conquered territory.

After Gaugamela, when there was essentially no competing paymaster, there seems to have been an explosion in the numbers of mercenaries enrolling with Alexander's army, to such an extent that both Arrian and Curtius agree that Alexander had 120,000 men with him for the invasion of

India, not all of whom were mercenaries of course. What follows is a table of all of the mercenary reinforcements that our sources record as being received by Alexander throughout his career:[100]

At Miletus	300 infantry	Arrian, 1.19.6
From Chios	3,000 infantry (Persian garrison)	Arrian, 2.13.5; Curtius, 4.5.18
At Sidon	4,000 Infantry (Probably left as Egyptian garrison)	Arrian, 2.20.5
At Memphis	400 cavalry 500 Thracian cavalry	Arrian, 3.5.1
At Susa	4,000 infantry from the Peloponnese 980 cavalry from the Peloponnese 3,500 Trallians 600 Thracian cavalry	Curtius, 5.1.41; Diodorus, 17.65.1
In Media	5,000 infantry 1,000 cavalry	Curtius, 5.7.12
	1,500 infantry (remnants of Darius' mercenaries)	Arrian, 3.23.8; Curtius, 6.5.6
	X number of infantry and cavalry from among the Greek allies who volunteered to remain with Alexander after their contingents had been demobilized.	Arrian, 3.19.6; Diodorus, 17.74.4
At Bactra	2,600 infantry 500 cavalry 3,000 Illyrian cavalry 300 cavalry	Curtius, 6.6.35
At Zariaspa	16,400 infantry 2,600 cavalry	Curtius, 6.10.11; Arrian, 4.7.2
In India	7,000 infantry 5,000 cavalry	Curtius, 9.3.21
	30,000 infantry 6,000 cavalry	Diodorus, 17.95.4
In Carmania	5,000 infantry 1,000 cavalry	Curtius, 10.1.1
At Babylon	Unknown	Arrian, 7.23.1

It should be noted that these are only the reinforcements that our sources record; it is highly likely that many more were received by Alexander that we hear nothing about. It is also true that many mercenaries were hired directly by the city or province in which they were to act as a garrison; therefore they would never have been part of the army itself and as a consequence would have largely escaped the notice of our sources. One thinks of the 20,000 mercenaries recruited by Peucestas, the satrap of Sardis, within one year of the demobilization decree of Alexander in 324. These troops were never part of the field army and thus are never counted towards troop totals but they were potentially available for use by Alexander as required.

Organization of the Mercenaries

Throughout Alexander's career, most particularly in his later years, there was an almost constant influx of new troops as existing ones were leaving the grand host to be assigned garrison duties. The organization of the mercenary contingent within Alexander's army was, by necessity, fluid and is difficult to pin down. There does, however, appear to be a terminological distinction preserved by Arrian who uses the word *xenoi* to refer to mercenaries that had been with the army from the outset, whilst the word *misthophoroi* refers to mercenaries subsequently recruited in Asia. This distinction generally works down to the Battle of Gaugamela, particularly with regard to the mercenary cavalry. The terms themselves are a little different: *misthophoroi* refers generally to mercenaries, while *xenoi* is usually taken to refer specifically to foreigners in the sense of people from another Greek city-state, not, for example, Persians or Egyptians. *Xenoi* did not appear to mean 'mercenary' originally, or have any military connotations, but Arrian adopts and adapts its use to suit his purpose.

At Gaugamela two bodies of mercenary cavalry are recorded: those who joined the army in Egypt, commanded by Menidas, are called *misthophoroi*; those under the command of Andromachus are called *xenoi*. It can be presumed that these were originally with the expeditionary force of Parmenio, as no mercenary cavalry are recorded with the army of invasion in Diodorus and no other reinforcements were recorded beside those in Egypt.[101]

Unfortunately the distinction in terminology is not universally true, as an examination of the mercenary infantry will demonstrate. *Misthophoroi* infantry are first mentioned just before the Battle of Issus: Parmenio is sent ahead of the main body with a small force, consisting of *misthophoroi*, the Thessalian cavalry and the Thracians. This incident is, however, too early for a significant number of *misthophoroi* to be present, given that the *misthophoroi* were supposed to be those recruited after the invasion. The only mercenary infantry to have been enlisted with the army to that point were the 300 from the garrison at Miletus, and this seems far too small a number to be taking part in the expedition that Arrian is describing – especially when compared to the other, significantly larger, contingents being used. It is much more likely that the mercenaries Parmenio took were all the Greek mercenaries with the army, a force of perhaps 5,000 men or more. The same problem recurs soon after this at the Battle of Issus, where there are two bodies of mercenary infantry mentioned. The *xenoi* can, of course, be explained as the remnants of the expeditionary force, but the 300 men from Miletus are still the only new recruits. Are we to believe that of these two bodies, one consisted of in excess of 5,000 men, the other only 300? I think not. It is far more likely that they were of roughly equal size given that they were performing a similar tactical function.

This superficially useful terminological distinction encounters another problem with the reinforcements received at Sidon. These were 4,000 in number and are the only known reinforcements to have reached the army before 331. These troops do not appear, however, in the Greek order of Battle at Gaugamela, and therefore must have been left on garrison duty at some unspecified location before that battle. The only logical place for a garrison of this size between Issus and Gaugamela is in Egypt, where, coincidentally enough, we know that Alexander left a garrison, 4,000 strong. Arrian calls the new recruits received at Sidon *misthophoroi*, as he should if the terminological theory is correct; but the troops left behind in Egypt are referred to as *xenoi*. If, however, the Egyptian garrison were *xenoi*, this does not solve the problem, as the reinforcements received at Sidon (the *misthophoroi*) are still not mentioned at Gaugamela, nor are they known to have been left on garrison duty anywhere else. The simplest answer to the problem of this use of terminology in Arrian is to assume that although the words could indicate a different origin for each batch of mercenaries, the distinction does not always hold true. Either it is a misunderstanding on the part of Arrian or of his sources; or perhaps the terms originally referred to the two separate bodies of mercenaries, but the distinction between them became confused, or was simply lost, as garrison duty and natural wastage reduced the size of both bodies. New recruits could be assigned to either *misthophoroi* or *xenoi* to keep the numbers at relatively stable levels. This also means that early in the campaign the distinction would be most valid, but would decline in relevance over time; this is exactly the pattern that we see in Arrian's usage of the terms.

The Role of Mercenary and Allied Troops

Mercenaries formed a fundamental and immensely important part of Alexander's army throughout the course of his career, despite their seeming lack of involvement in the set-piece battles. Their versatility can be summed by a consideration of their various roles:

- Secondary Columns
- Garrisons
- Front Line Troops
- Colonies
- Hostages

Each of these roles was vital to the overall success of the campaign but generally is overlooked as focus is usually upon the set-piece battles where the Macedonian native troops were the most important, along with the Thessalian cavalry of course. Each of the above roles will be considered separately.

Secondary Columns

Before 331, Alexander, with very few exceptions, kept his Macedonian troops with him. If any areas needed to be conquered that were not directly on his marching route, a secondary column would be detached to deal with these threats. These columns were often, although not exclusively, commanded by Parmenio, as with the column sent by Alexander to Magnesia and Tralles when the main body was at Ephesus. This column is particularly interesting as Arrian states that it consisted of 2,500 mercenaries, 2,500 Macedonians and 200 Companion Cavalry. This force seems excessively large as the two cities had already offered their joint surrender, and so this can not have been an army of conquest, but rather one of occupation. The mercenaries can be explained as they were probably intended for garrison duty; this does not explain, however, the presence of so many Macedonians. This difficulty is compounded by Arrian a few lines further in his text when he states that a similar force was sent to the Aeolian towns and all the Ionian cities still subject to Persia. This equally considerable force was under the command of Alcimachus. It seems highly unlikely that Alexander would have detached 5,000 Macedonian heavy infantry and 400 Companion Cavalry to conduct these relatively minor operations at the very outset of the campaign. This is especially the case when we consider that he was unsure how swiftly the Persians could regroup, or even whether the Persian force at the Granicus was designed to slow his advance in anticipation of Darius' arrival, rather than to defeat him itself. It would seem reasonable for Alexander to have assumed that the Ionian cities would come over to him without a fight, and so sending the elite troops of his army on these expeditions would seem unnecessary, thus only small numbers of satellite forces were used.

How then, do we deal with this problem? Either Alexander did not do what we may reasonably have expected, or Arrian is wrong. In this instance I believe the latter to be true. I suspect that when Arrian mentions Macedonians he was actually referring to a contingent of Alexander's Balkan allies, an easy enough mistake perhaps, especially when we realize that he calls the second detachment a 'similar force', not mentioning the Macedonians directly and therefore perhaps not noticing his earlier error. This argument is supported by the fact that neither the Illyrian nor the Thracian allied contingents are mentioned as being present on the march to Miletus.[102] What the Companion Cavalry were on these expeditions is more difficult to ascertain: they either were what they appear to be, or they were *prodromoi*. Given that the *prodromoi* were later incorporated into the Companion Cavalry *ilai*, it is reasonable enough to assume a careless error by Arrian here. There is also no mention of them being present with the army at Arrian 1.18.3.

These secondary columns were, however, not always successful in their assigned tasks. When Satibarzanes and Spitamenes revolted in Asia, Alexander sent two expeditions. The first, sent against Satibarzanes, consisted entirely of mercenaries – this can be assumed as both commanders (Erigyius and Andronicus) were mercenaries themselves –

and was wholly successful; on the other hand, the expedition sent against Spitamenes was not. This second expedition consisted of 60 Companion Cavalry, 800 mercenary cavalry and 1,500 mercenary infantry, under the overall command of Pharnuches, a Lydian. This represents a significant break from the norm, in that a non-Macedonian was commanding Macedonian troops. Curtius and Arrian give different accounts of how the disaster came about but both represent it as a crushing blow. Neither account apportions any blame to the mercenary troops; it is most likely that the fault lay either with the individual commanders, or more probably with the unsound method of appointing a native civilian to the leadership of a military expedition. One imagines that this latter sentiment would have been felt by the Macedonians; they were always unwilling to accept foreigners, either in command as here, or within their own ranks, as with the Persian cavalry joining the various *ilai* of the Companions.

The very nature of some of these secondary columns also changed after 331. Several times a relatively small group, consisting usually of Macedonians, was detached and led by Alexander himself, whilst the main body of the army, along with the baggage train, proceeded along safer paths. However, this change probably had more to do with Alexander's need for conquest and personal glory, and his crushing boredom when inactive, rather than any judgment on his behalf as to the relative effectiveness of the mercenary troops left behind. For example, in 331/0, Parmenio was given command of the main body of the army with orders to proceed along the main road towards Pasargadae, whilst Alexander campaigned against the Uxii with his Macedonians and Agrianians. A further example is Alexander's final pursuit of Darius.

Garrisons

One of the most important roles the mercenaries played within the empire that Alexander was creating was that of garrison troops. Virtually all of the fighting troops in the expanding Macedonian Empire that were not part of the immediate entourage of the king were mercenaries. Most of the cities that Alexander captured were left a garrison of mercenaries, for example Ephesus, Halicarnassus, Mytilene, Miletus, Egypt: the list of garrisoned towns is, of course, as extensive as Alexander's newly-forming empire.

The first certain example of a garrison that is of significant size is that of Caria. Alexander left Halicarnassus after only a week-long siege (having captured only one of the three citadels); leaving behind 3,000 troops, under the command of Ptolemy, to complete the reduction of the city. The siege of Halicarnassus was certainly not Alexander's finest hour. It is my belief, however, that he abandoned it so quickly, before its capture was complete, because his newly-formulated naval policy made it essential that he capture all the major Persian ports with as little delay as possible. Why Alexander left this major Persian port unconquered, after he stated the policy of defeating the Persian fleet on land, is something of a mystery. It may be due to his overwhelming desire to progress further into Asia: a lengthy siege at this stage of his campaign was simply an unwanted delay to the young king. We are told nothing more about the organisation of a mercenary garrison of Caria, save that Ada was appointed civilian governor of the region. In order to learn more we must move on to the next great employment of mercenaries: Egypt.

Egypt provides us with the best view of the military organization of a province within Alexander's empire; it was a model that was to be repeated many times, as we shall see. Alexander appointed two native Egyptian governors, and two Companion cavalrymen to act as commanders of the Macedonian garrisons at Memphis and Pelusium.[103] Lycidas, a Greek, was given command of the mercenary forces throughout the province. Alexander also appointed a 'secretary of foreign troops', these being the mercenaries, and two commissioners. The mercenaries appear to have been rather overstaffed, with four separate officers. A second problem is that Curtius seems to have the view that Aeschylus, one of the commissioners, and Peucestas, the military commander, are of the same status, apparently regarding Aeschylus as the administrative head of Egypt.[104] We cannot be certain, however, that the mercenary troops were 'overstaffed' as we have very little evidence of the organization of any other provinces, and even less with regard to the organization of mercenaries (or allies) in the main army. This administrative situation may well be completely normal; there were 4,000 mercenaries after all, and only two small Macedonian garrisons requiring fewer officers. There is a possibility that the two commissioners, or as he calls them inspectors of the mercenaries, were in fact there to oversee the civilian governors and in reality had little to do with the troops.[105] This seems to be an eminently-plausible suggestion. This would also parallel the later situation in eastern Iran where Tlepolemus and Neiloxenus oversaw the work of the native satraps. If Egypt was assigned a greater number of governors, military officers and so on, then this would simply be an indication of the importance of that satrapy. Egypt had been the source of constant difficulty to the Persians, and Alexander did not want to encounter the same problems. Egypt was also a major source of grain for the Greek world, as it was to become for Rome, and no doubt the same is true for the army too, at least while campaigning in the western Persian Empire.

Front-line Troops

The Macedonian elements in the army of course played the leading roles in each of Alexander's set-piece battles; but we should not overlook the contributions made by the mercenary troops. At the Battle of the River Granicus, neither the mercenaries nor the allied troops are mentioned at all. This should not worry us too much as the Granicus was a relatively small battle, certainly in comparison to Issus, Gaugamela and the Hydaspes that is. However the question remains: what were they doing at the time of the battle? The only answers can be either that they were away from the main body of the army, yet still playing some role in the fighting; or they were away on some secondary mission; or perhaps that they formed a reserve or second line which is not mentioned because it was not called into use. I find this latter argument to be the more likely considering their later roles at Issus and Gaugamela. Their function in these later battles was to prevent the army from being outflanked and to protect the rear of the Macedonian heavy infantry units. Alexander was evidently a man who reused successful tactics, albeit adapted to individual circumstances, and the provision of a reserve line would seem a sensible insurance policy against the battle not going entirely as planned.

At Issus the picture is a little clearer; Alexander drew up his heavy infantry facing the Persians, with the Companion Cavalry to the right of the infantry. A strong flank guard was assigned to the right wing, where the Persian line overlapped his own. It seems that he deployed the mercenary troops on the left, along with the Peloponnesians and the rest of the allied cavalry. A curious decision, as they were essentially hoplites assigned to the sandy area next to the sea, terrain most suited to a charge by the Persian cavalry. Alexander seems to have soon realized his error and sent the Thessalian cavalry to the left wing. What then happened to the mercenaries

1. The so-called 'Alexander Mosaic' from Pompeii, showing Alexander the Great leading a cavalry charge into the flank of the Persians around Darius (in his chariot), while the long sarissae of the phalanx can be seen approaching from the front. The detail (inset) depicts Alexander wearing a breastplate very similar to the one found at Vergina. He is shown without a helmet so his features can be seen; helmets were certainly worn by the Macedonian cavalry. (Photo copyright of Rien van der Weijgaert)

2. Breastplate decorated in gold, found in Tomb II at Vergina. It is of almost identical design to that worn by Alexander on the 'Alexander Mosaic'. (Courtesy of Triandafyllos Papazois at www.tdpapazois.gr)

3. Hilt of the sword found in Tomb II at Vergina. It is heavily decorated in gold and ivory and probably originates from Cyprus. (Courtesy of Triandafyllos Papazois at www.tdpapazois.gr)

4. and 5. A reconstruction of a Macedonian phalangite and a traditional hoplite. The *pelta* shield of the *pezhetairoi* would have been a little more concave than the reconstruction, but the difference between the sizes of the *sarissa* and the hoplite spear is apparent. The reach advantage this gave to the Macedonians is demonstrated below. Note the neck strap for the *pelta* allowing the *sarissa* to be held in both hands.
(Photo courtesy of Ryan Jones; Macedonian equipment modelled by Paul Dunn, hoplite panoply by Jeff Melcher)

6. Replica of the most common style of cuirass in the 4th century. Made of layers of stiffened linen or leather, sometimes reinforced with panels of metal scales, such armour would have been worn by Alexander's heavy infantry (those that wore any at all) and many of the Greek mercenaries and allies. Compare with plates 14, 15, 16 and 22.

7. A Phrygian helmet of the type worn in the Macedonian army of the fourth century, now in the Art Institute of Chicago.
(Image courtesy of Jasper Oorthuys of Ancient Warfare Magazine)

8. Replicas of the head of a Macedonian *sarissa* and the fluted butt spike that helped to counterbalance it. (Courtesy of www.manningimperial.com).

9. Replica fourth-century *kopis* sword; this type was not as common as the traditional straight hoplite sword but was also employed by the Macedonians. (Courtesy of www.deepeeka.co.in)

10. Replica of a fourth-century Greek sword of the more common, straight type. (Courtesy of www.deepeeka.co.in)

11. Replica hoplite spear head and butt; these are identical to those used by the Macedonian heavy infantry when conditions made the use of the *sarissa* impossible, and traditional hoplite spears were employed. (Courtesy of www.deepeeka.co.in)

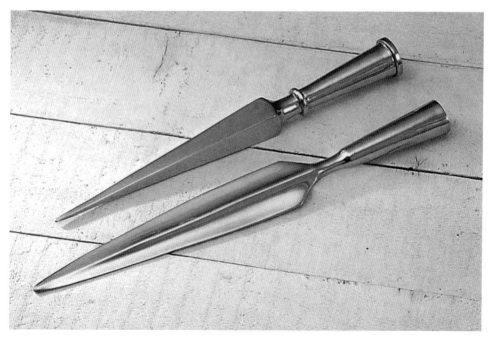

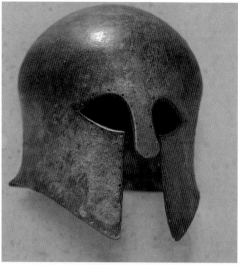

12. Two-part bronze cuirass, with sculpted musculature, circa 350-300, from southern Italy, now in the British Museum. This is of a type worn by some traditional hoplites, not by Macedonian *pezhetairoi*. (Courtesy of Marie-Lan Nguyen/Wikimedia Commons)

13. A standard traditional Corinthian helmet of the type worn by the mercenaries and allies, now in the Louvre, Paris; a very different design to the Phrygian helmet of the Macedonian infantry. (Courtesy of Marie-Lan Nguyen/Wikimedia Commons)

14. Traditional hoplites clash on this fragment from the podium frieze on the Nereid Monument at Xanthos in Lycia, from the fourth century, now in the British Museum. Note the size of the shield and the strap on the inside; the *pelta* used by the Macedonian heavy infantry would have hung from the neck, although a strap would also have been present to manoeuvre the shield while in use. (Courtesy of Marie-Lan Nguyen/Wikimedia Commons)

15. A scene on the pediment of the so-called 'Alexander Sarcophagus' from Sidon, now in the Archaeological Museum of Istanbul. The infantrymen in the centre and left are Macedonians; note the Phrygian helmets and the style of cuirass. They appear to be depicted with the large traditional hoplite shield, not the smaller *pelta* carried when the *sarissa* was used. The bearded figure on the right wears a traditional muscled cuirass and is probably an allied or mercenary Greek hoplite. (Photo copyright of Dick Osseman)

16. A detail from the sarcophagus' famous battle scene, showing Alexander's infantry and cavalry in action against the Persians. Note the Phrygian helmet of the Macedonian infantryman and the Boeotian helmet of the cavalryman. (Photo copyright of Wayne Boucher)

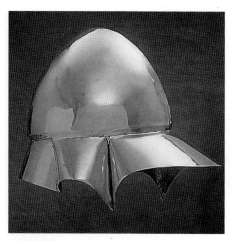

17. A replica of Boeotian helmet like those worn by the Macedonian cavalry on the Alexander Sarcophagus (Courtesy of www.deepeeka.co.in)

18. Another detail from the battle scene on the sarcophagus, showing a Macedonian Companion cavalryman, with cuirass, Boeotian helmet and straight sword. He would originally have been striking with a lance, which, like all the weapons, is unfortunately now missing. (Photo copyright of Wayne Boucher)

19. A detail of the hunting scene from the other side of the sarcophagus, showing Macedonians and newly-conquered Persians working together. In the ancient world hunting played the same role as team sports do today in forming a bond of friendship and trust between individuals, thus bolstering morale on the battlefield. (Photo copyright of Wayne Boucher)

20. Possible appearance of an Agrianian javelin man. Note the multiple spears being carried for extra firepower. (Courtesy of Johnny Shumate)

21. One of the finest surviving stele paintings of a fourth-century Macedonian Companion cavalryman. Note the flowing cloak, the sheathed sword slung on the left side and the lance in his right hand.

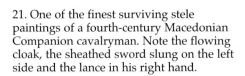

22. Another grave stele painting from early Ptolemaic Egypt, not long after the death of Alexander. The style of armour is clearly seen and his shield rests against something in the background.

is unclear: they could have occupied a position between the Thessalian cavalry and the Macedonian heavy infantry, similar to the role played by the hypaspists on the right of the line; they may have occupied a position on the far right of the line, which is equally unlikely; or they may have been withdrawn from the front to form part of a second line. The sources do not provide us with enough information to answer this directly; the confusion results from Arrian's use of the word *'epitasso'*, which can mean 'station', either alongside or behind.[106] The context of the passage would seem to make it clear that here it has to mean that the mercenaries were placed behind everybody else. The other interpretation would have the mercenaries, a medium-heavy infantry division, on the extreme left of the whole army, where it was Alexander's practice to put his Thessalian cavalry and some light infantry support. It seems certain then that Alexander used a second line, what some may call a tactical reserve, at the Battle of Issus.

The role of the allied infantry supplied by the League of Corinth, and of the Balkan allies, is more difficult to ascertain. They are not mentioned in any of the sources as forming the second line at Issus or Gaugamela alongside the mercenaries. They were surely far too numerous to have been left behind to guard the baggage train, however. Arrian's order of battle is not exhaustive for this campaign: the Odrysian cavalry and Balacrus' javelinmen are not mentioned either, and so the absence is no doubt an omission by Arrian and not some deeper mystery that could have us inventing another campaign or some elaborate tactic simply to explain away their absence. The mercenaries and allies therefore seemed to form a tactically important second line. It should be understood that by 'second line' we mean something distinct from the front line: not simply a group of troops that attached themselves to the back of the heavy infantry *taxeis*, but an entirely separate line with a distinct tactical role, as discussed below.

Gaugamela provides us with the best evidence for the combat role of the mercenary and allied troops. Alexander laid out his heavy infantry, Companion Cavalry and Thessalian cavalry according to his standard plan; which is to say with the Thessalians to the extreme left, heavy infantry in the centre, hypaspists to their right and Companion Cavalry to the extreme right of the line. This is the general formation that was adapted at almost every opportunity. The *prodromoi* and a number of other minor contingents were positioned to the right of the Companions, with Menidas' mercenary cavalry to the extreme right of the formation and Cleander's mercenary infantry behind them. On the left of the formation were Sitalces' Thracian infantry and three bodies of allied or League cavalry along with Andromachos' mercenary horse.

A second line of infantry was positioned parallel to the front: it consisted of the allied troops supplied from the League of Corinth and a smaller number of Balkan allies and mercenaries not stationed elsewhere. In order to form the hollow 'square' that was required, Cleander's mercenaries, the Agrianians and the archers were stationed to the right. They were in contact with the front line and spread out at approximately a 45 degree angle behind it. A corresponding position on the left was filled by Sitalces' Thracian infantry. The formation that resulted would have looked like a blunt arrow head. The formation was further complicated by the fact that the second line only extended about halfway along the formation, starting from the left wing, resulting in the right hand half of the front line having no second line troops positioned behind it. This is suggested by the fact that when a small group of Bactrian cavalry broke through the front line, they met no further resistance before reaching Alexander's camp. The mercenary and allied troops that formed the second line at Gaugamela were positioned in order that if Alexander's position were turned – highly likely given the discrepancy in numbers - he would not automatically be defeated. The second line could simply turn around and fight with their backs to the front line. They were stationed there, in short, to ensure that if the battle did not go well, Alexander could still win. Their ability to perform this function was not seriously tested but that should not detract from the potential importance of this role.

Colonies

After 331, when Alexander began to enter the northeastern parts of the former Persian Empire, his mercenary and allied troops were to become increasingly important. In this region Alexander founded a series of colonies, although they were probably rather fewer in number than was believed a few decades ago.[107] This was a move perhaps partly designed to spread Greek culture, although this should not be over emphasized as this was very much a by-product of their presence in these regions and not their primary function. They were primarily designed to help pacify the outer parts of the empire. It was to be hoped that these new foundations, which were, essentially, military colonies, would act as a calming influence on the always – potentially – rebellious natives. These colonies, then, had a largely strategic rather than a tactical function. They were also partly forced upon Alexander because he had ever-increasing numbers of troops who were past service and needed to be pensioned off. The best attested evidence for a colony that we have is Alexandria in Caucaso, the modern Begram in the central Hindu Kush Mountains, at the confluence of the Gorband and Panjshir rivers. Here Alexander established a city with a nucleus of 3,000 Graeco-Macedonian settlers, soldiers no longer fit for service, and volunteers from among the mercenaries, together with 7,000 of the local population. This became something of a standard pattern, a blend of native and Graeco-Macedonian settlers. Alexander no doubt hoped that, if there was a native revolt, these retired troops would act to suppress it, and that as a by-product of their presence they would also spread Greek culture to the furthest reaches of the known world. This later point would be an added bonus that came with the foundation of the cities, rather than a primary purpose. These cities were essentially garrison towns and administrative centres.

Later evidence suggests that these Greeks were far from being the willing settlers that our sources portray them as being. On two separate occasions they themselves effectively revolted against Alexander. The first revolt occurred in Bactria when rumour spread that Alexander had died on the Indus. Some of the Greeks revolted under the banner of Athenodorus with the express intent of returning to Greece. This insurrection, however, fell in upon itself, with Athenodorus being assassinated by Biton, who was in turn tortured for such an act by the Greek settlers themselves. Diodorus' account of the fate of these 3,000 rebels is obscure, but Curtius has them eventually getting home.[108]

This small revolt was the precursor to a much larger one that occurred after Alexander's death. It seems the Greeks were not at all happy with being left on the edge of the civilized world; they longed for home, just as the Macedonians evidently did at the Opis revolt.

Hostages

It may seem slightly odd to include something with such a negative connotation amongst the roles played by the allied, although not the mercenary, troops, but it was an important one. The main reason that

Alexander had for including 7,000 Balkan allies at the outset of the expedition was not to increase his number of front-line troops, but to remove a significant number of young men from a potentially-dangerous region of Europe: dangerous for Antipater that is. Many of these Odrysians, Thracians, Illyrians etc, would have remembered the time when they were free from Macedonian rule in their very recent past, and, with the absence of Alexander and the main part of the Macedonian army in Asia, they might very easily have been persuaded to revolt.

The same argument can be applied to the troops supplied by the League of Corinth. If they had been allowed to remain in Greece, the Persians could quite easily have created rebellion at home, which may very well have been Memnon's strategy at the time of his death in 334. We should also note that the League supplied Alexander with a number of ships (Alexander's fleet will be discussed in a separate chapter).

The allies' main function on the expedition seems to have been to act as a guarantor of the good behaviour of their home states: they are seldom used as front line troops, as discussed above, and are seldom left as garrisons. One instance where allied troops are left behind is in 330, when the troops left at Ecbatana with Parmenio consisted of Greek mercenaries, Thracians and non-Macedonian cavalry. The only instance recorded of League troops on garrison duty is the contingent from Argos assigned to garrison Sardis. They are always kept close to Alexander; their loyalty, it would seem, was questionable.

Did Alexander Trust His Mercenary and Allied Troops?

It would seem appropriate to look at this question in two parts, first considering the allied troops, then the mercenaries, as separate entities. As stated above, it seems that the primary reason for the presence of the Balkan troops and those supplied by the League of Corinth was to act as hostages. Removing large numbers of young men from the native populations, young men who had in all likelihood fought against Philip or Alexander in the recent past, would tend to pacify those regions of Greece. The question of trust is far more complex than this, though. The allied troops were numerically very strong indeed: 7,000 supplied by the League of Corinth and a further 7,000 Thracians, Triballians and Illyrians. These 14,000 troops could easily have caused Alexander's defeat at Issus or

Gaugamela if they had chosen to switch sides during the height of the battle, but they did not. I am of course assuming here that the allied troops did take some part in these two battles, most likely as part of a reserve line. If they did form part of a second line, behind the Macedonian front, then they were supremely positioned to attack the Macedonians in the rear, which would have led to certain defeat: the fact that they did not speaks to their having some degree of loyalty to Alexander. Counter to this argument is the fact that Alexander seldom seems to have let them out of his sight. They are rarely used as garrison troops, and equally seldom used to form parts of subsidiary expeditions: League of Corinth troops are only mentioned under the command of Parmenio in the Troad, at the Amanus Gates, in Phrygia and in the march on Persis.[109]

It would seem, then, that although the opportunity for disloyalty did present itself, the fact that they did not act upon it is suggestive of a certain degree of loyalty. Yet this sense of loyalty may very well not have sprung from a positive source: it could have been out of fear of reprisals against their home states by Alexander's regent, Antipater.

Darius and Memnon seem to have made a significant strategic error in not (as far as we know) seeking to exploit any anti-Macedonian sentiment. However, if Memnon had lived longer, and carried the war on to mainland Greece, we could very well have seen the expedition fall into serious difficulties. Whether Alexander would have turned back at all is another point entirely: he does not seem to have been too concerned by the affairs of Greece, for example during the revolt of Agis of Sparta.

The mercenaries present a different problem: they were with the expedition out of choice and not because of some political hold Alexander may have had over their home city-states. Their reasons for any potential disloyalty would, therefore, have been very different from that of the allied troops. Disloyalty among mercenaries is often on financial rather than political grounds, after all. The only real evidence, if we can call it evidence, for the hypothesis that Alexander did not trust his mercenary troops is that Curtius records an attempt by Darius to 'buy off' some of Alexander's mercenaries. It seems that a letter from Darius to an unnamed recipient was intercepted, some time just before the Battle of Gaugamela. In this letter, Darius was attempting to sow the seeds of dissension among Alexander's mercenary troops; Alexander was in favour of reading the letter to a general assembly of troops but was persuaded out of this course of action by Parmenio who stated that that Alexander was 'vulnerable even if only one man were a traitor'.[110] Parmenio, then, seems to have had potential doubts over the loyalty of some mercenaries too, but the ultimate proof is simply that they were never actually disloyal. The obvious exception is those 'volunteers' who had been settled in the northeast of the empire and rebelled in order to get home, not whilst with the main army or whilst they were attached to secondary columns. This only occurred firstly when they believed Alexander to be dead and secondly when Alexander had actually died. They had far greater opportunities for rebellion than the allies did as they had far more wide-reaching roles, for instance as garrisons in every key city Alexander captured. The real reason that Alexander did not make great use of his mercenaries and allies was not that he did not trust them, but simply that they were trained and equipped to perform a different role from that which the Macedonian heavy infantry were trained. Many of the mercenaries would have been heavily-armed hoplites, troops that simply did not fit with the Macedonian style of combat that required troops that were more mobile and flexible. They were useful in limited roles, but not in set-piece battles.

Demobilization Decree

Soon after leaving the Gedrosian Desert, Alexander issued one of the most controversial decrees of his career: he ordered all of his satraps in Asia to disband their mercenary armies. The only source that mentions this decree is Diodorus, and he does so only briefly. He tells us that Alexander had come to realize that several of his satraps had 'acted arbitrarily and selfishly', and that some of his governors had committed 'serious offences'.[111] Upon the satraps realizing that Alexander was becoming aware of their feathering their own nests, rather than governing in the interests of Alexander and the new Macedonian Empire, several of the satraps revolted and others fled with as much money as they could. Diodorus tells us:[112]

> As news of this was brought to the king, he wrote to all of his generals and satraps in Asia, ordering them, as soon as they had read his letter, to disband all their mercenaries instantly.

Diodorus sets this decree in the context of Alexander's attempts to suppress certain satraps who had been acting more as despots than subordinates to the king. There is a precedent to this decree: in 359/8

Artaxerxes III instructed his western satraps to disband their mercenaries, thereby precipitating the revolt of Artabazus. Artaxerxes' decree was a security measure and Diodorus presents Alexander's decree in the same light, but I would tentatively argue that there is more to Alexander's decree than security.

Alexander did not simply demobilize these troops; he did not intend them to disappear, or to return home to Greece, that would have been unrealistic in the extreme, although some have argued that that is exactly what happened and that the decree may have been specifically intended to repopulate the depleted Greek cities.[113] Tens of thousands of men who had been mercenaries all or most of their adult lives would not simply have returned to Greece to become farmers: they would, in all likelihood, have caused great problems for Alexander. Alexander, I believe, did not intend to disband these mercenaries; instead, he may have intended them to become part of his field army. If this is indeed the case then it is therefore misleading to speak of demobilization, as the troops were to be transferred from the satraps to the mobile field army. Greek mercenary troops acted as garrisons in every major town and city throughout the empire, and their demobilization would suggest that the satrapies were to be left relatively defenceless against internal uprisings. This would have been a situation that Alexander would never have allowed. If it had been Alexander's intent to demobilize these mercenaries completely and leave the satraps with no garrisons, then we should see evidence of this in the sources and we do not. In fact we see the exact opposite. We know for example that Peucestas, who was appointed to the satrapy of Persis in early 324, raised an army in excess of 20,000 strong within a year of taking up his position.[114] If Peucestas raised a very strong army within a remarkably-short period of time, we can safely assume that others did too. We know with some certainty, therefore, that satrapal armies were not outlawed.

If the intention was for the 'demobilized' mercenaries to join the grand host, we must ask why Alexander would require such a huge injection of new troops. Alexander's reserves of mercenaries must have been very low at this point in the campaign, following the demands of his city foundations in India, the constant need for garrisons and the severe losses in the Gedrosian Desert disaster. It seems to me, therefore, that this decree was not a reactive measure to prevent the possibility of revolt, as Diodorus would suggest, but a proactive one. Alexander was using the mercenaries that were already at his disposal in the satrapal armies to replenish his army of the losses that they had incurred in the previous year or two. The satraps would then be allowed to rebuild their forces at their own leisure: they had the time, Alexander did not. Some satraps seem to have misunderstood this decree – those who evidently had been exploiting their positions for personal gain. This decree, then, led to several satraps revolting; it was not the case that these revolts led to the decree.

Chapter 6

Mediterranean Fleets

—⁊⁊—

It may at first sight appear strange to use the word 'fleet' in the plural rather than the singular in the title of this chapter, but I do so deliberately. There is no doubt that Alexander possessed more than one fleet during the early years of the invasion: he did in fact possess four.

The Fleet of the League of Corinth

One of the burdens placed on the members of the League of Corinth after the allied Greek defeat at Chaeronea, and subsequent recognition of Macedonian hegemony, was to supply ships to aid the war effort. This fleet was established in 336 or shortly before, and its main purpose was to act as support to the land operations being conducted by the field army. This support largely involved them acting as transports and maintaining the lines of supply and communication with Macedonia and Greece. The fleet must have been remarkably heterogeneous and was of moderate size, consisting of 160 ships of which a mere 20 were supplied by the strongest naval power in Greece: Athens. At this time the Athenians had around 300 ships in commission; the supply of only 20 is perhaps suggestive of their level of enthusiasm for Alexander's expedition. Many of the smaller city-states would have supplied the merest handful. Arrian tells us that the fleet was untrained, each member state evidently only sending the worst ships and sailors at its disposal, simply to honour a commitment.[115] The resulting fleet was effectively useless as a fighting force; it was poorly trained and consisted of large numbers of contingents who had never fought as a cohesive unit before. Coupled to this was Alexander's total lack of knowledge of naval operations. Realistically it would have been impossible for Alexander to have operated with anything but the most basic tactics.

This is strongly suggested by Arrian when he has Alexander, in debate with Parmenio as to whether to engage the Persian fleet at sea, saying that he would 'not risk making a present to the Persians of all the skill and courage of his men'.[116]

This can only be a reference to the potential loss of Macedonian troops, not Greek sailors, and suggests that Alexander's naval tactics would rely on boarding Persian ships and fighting hand to hand. This would effectively be to fight a land battle at sea. These tactics are not wholly surprising in a commander who had no experience at all of naval warfare, either directly or through Philip's tutelage. The tactics that Alexander likely would have employed are, interestingly, exactly how the Vikings fought their naval battles.

Despite the evidently poor quality of vessels supplied by his allies, Alexander's Greek fleet had proved itself of greater use than simply for logistics and transport alone. Whilst Alexander was besieging the city of Miletus by land, the Persian fleet of some 400 vessels was heading north to relieve it. If the Persians had arrived, the city could presumably have held out against the Macedonians almost indefinitely, as reinforcements and supplies could easily be transported by sea. Nicanor, commander of Alexander's Greek fleet, arrived three days before the Persians, however, and anchored his vessels off the Milesian coast on the island of Lade.[117] The Persian fleet, unable to find any port suitable to meet its supply needs, and seemingly unable or unwilling to engage the Greeks in these narrow waters, set sail south again. Thus Alexander's fleet had proved, quite convincingly, that, despite his unwillingness to offer a naval battle, his fleet could still be of considerable military usefulness. This makes the subsequent decision to disband it even more baffling.

Soon after the capture of Miletus, and before the commencement of operations at Halicarnassus, Alexander made one of the most debated decisions of his career: he disbanded his fleet. Arrian gives us five reasons:[118]

- Lack of money.
- The Persian navy was far superior to Alexander's own.
- Alexander was unwilling to risk any losses, in ships or men, in a naval engagement.
- Alexander believed that he no longer needed a fleet as he was now master of the continent of Asia.

• He intended to defeat the Persian navy on land by depriving it of its ports.

Lack of money is the reason most commonly accepted by modern historians as the major factor in Alexander's decision; it is also the *only* reason cited by Diodorus.[119] The conclusion that the decision was financially motivated is flawed for two reasons. Firstly, the fleet was supplied by the member states of the League of Corinth; it is therefore reasonable to assume that the cost of their upkeep would also fall on these states and not on Alexander. The fleet would, effectively, have cost him almost nothing to maintain. Secondly, Alexander should not have been short of funds at this point. Just a few months later at Gordium, during the winter of 334/3, Alexander invested 500 talents on raising a new fleet and 600 talents were allotted to pay for the upkeep of garrisons on the Greek mainland.[120] There seems no reason why Alexander's financial position should have improved so drastically in just a few short months, we know of no major Persian treasuries in this area that had fallen into Alexander's hands.

Arrian is correct to say that the Persian fleet was superior to Alexander's, both in numbers and quality. This is not a reason to demobilize the fleet, however, as this would leave the islands and the mainland defenceless from a naval assault. Miletus had also shown Alexander that a fleet was tactically useful even if he did not offer battle to the Persians. This lack of quality and numbers would be more of an argument for increasing investment in the fleet, rather than ridding himself of it.

Arrian's second and third points are certainly linked; Alexander was unwilling to offer a naval battle because of the potential ramifications. His strategy would involve a heavy reliance on marines, most likely the hypaspists, given that these were the most versatile heavy infantry troops that he commanded. These were also the troops that were assigned to the final naval assault against Tyre, so it is most likely that they would have been chosen for this mission too. Yet he needed every one of these troops for the land campaign, making a naval campaign even more problematic. Any defeat could also have caused political problems back in Greece too; it would have been an open invitation for general rebellion throughout Greece.

The suggestion by Arrian that Alexander did not need a fleet, as he already controlled the whole continent, is extraordinary and obviously not true. Even if we take Arrian to be referring to Asia Minor, rather than the whole of Asia, then it still was nowhere near true. Besides, there was now nothing stopping the Persians from attacking Alexander's forces in the rear, which they in fact did at Tenedos.[121] This was a tactic that should have been employed far more effectively than it ever was by the Persians.

This strategy of defeating the Persian navy on land is famous, and, on the surface, fairly sound. In the ancient world warships could not carry any great quantity of supplies and so had to dock at a friendly port every night to resupply themselves with food and fresh water. It is also true that this strategy ultimately worked: the Persian fleet did collapse as Alexander captured key cities on the Phoenician coast. Yet the strategy had at least two serious flaws. The first was that a competent commander, as Memnon surely was, had a free hand to act as he wished in the Aegean; to overrun all of the islands and carry the fight to the mainland where several states would more than likely have revolted given the opportunity. The second was that it does not take any account of the fact that a significant portion of the Persian fleet was from Cyprus, which would theoretically have been unaffected by this strategy; although these ships would still have needed mainland ports in order to operate, they would still be loyal to the Persians and able to harass Alexander's rear with Alexander having no possibility of using his land army to capture their ports. Alexander essentially relied upon luck to overcome these two problems, which was very uncharacteristic. His planning was usually far more meticulous than this and his strategies were well thought out, which leads me to conclude that his decision here was not a purely tactical or strategic one, but something rather different.

If the decision to disband the fleet was not taken on military grounds, nor forced upon him by lack of funds or any of the other reasons Arrian cites, why did he make this decision? I suspect that the truth lies in something that Arrian comes close to mentioning. He points out that any loss in battle could lead to disaffection and potential rebellion at home, bringing up the question of loyalty. I argued in an earlier chapter that the allied troops with the army were loyal to Alexander, although this could have been because of a fear of reprisals at home if they had rebelled. It could also have been because of the presence of thousands of heavily armed, battle-hardened Macedonians. The fleet would very quickly have been far away from the location of the king or the army, so Alexander's personality and influence would have had far less of an impact on them and the opportunity for disloyalty would have been exponentially greater, as well as being far easier to act upon. The fact that he retained the 20 Athenian vessels is an indication that he wanted to try to retain some specifically Athenian hostages, but 160 vessels was too great a risk.[122] It is interesting to note that all Alexander ever got from the great naval power of Athens were these 20 vessels along with 200 cavalry; these 20 vessels and their crew, then, were important hostages against the good behaviour of Athens.

The Fleet of Proteas

We know very little about this fleet, or indeed its commander, Proteas. We do know that whilst Alexander was at Gordium in the winter of 334/3, Antipater gave orders for the reconstruction of a Greek fleet. The fleet was raised principally on the island of Euboea and in the Peloponnese, and its primary purpose was to act as a defensive force against the possibility of Persian naval action against the islands or even the mainland. We know very little about the size of this fleet: Arrian simply says 'a number of warships' and the only evidence we have of it in action involved fifteen ships attacking a force of ten Persian vessels off the island of Siphnos. The fleet seems to have been in commission only until 332.[123]

The Fleet of Hegelochus and Amphoterus

There is only one reference in Arrian to the construction of a Macedonian national fleet, but we know from Curtius that whilst Alexander was marching between Gordium and Ancyra in the summer of 333 he invested 500 talents in the construction of just such a fleet.[124] This fleet was led by Hegelochus and Amphoterus, but it is evident from Arrian that Hegelochus was in supreme command. Curtius tells us specifically that the former was in charge of the troops and the latter was responsible for the ships and therefore, presumably, their crews.[125] It seems a slight contradiction that the commander of the naval element of a fleet was subordinate to the commander of the marines, but in reality none existed. It was not uncommon in the ancient world for this to be the arrangement and it is even less surprising when we consider the wider situation with Alexander, in which the army was the totally dominant military force. We also know, however, that Amphoterus was capable of acting independently when assignments arose: for example, he was sent to Lesbos, Chios and Cos at the head of a detachment of the fleet in 332.[126] When the Macedonian fleet joined Alexander in Egypt during the winter of 332/1 Hegelochus was reassigned, but we do not know where to. At this time Amphoterus assumed command of both the ships and the marines. The fleet then appears to have been operating off Crete and the Peloponnese. The fleet was decommissioned in 331.[127]

The Cypro-Phoenician Fleet

During the siege of Tyre in 333, soon after the mole was partially destroyed by the Tyrian fireship, Alexander along with his hypaspists and Agrianians set off on a mission to Sidon. Arrian tells us that this mission was 'in order to assemble there all the warships he possessed'.[128] It is unclear what this line actually means. It could be that Alexander intended to summon his Greek and Macedonian fleets to him; if this were the case, however, there was no need to travel to Sidon, and secondly there is no evidence that any such summons was issued or acted upon by the fleets.

It is perhaps more likely that Alexander believed quite simply that, as he now possessed the ports of Sidon and Byblos, along with many others, he also owned their fleets; he therefore travelled to Sidon to await their arrival home at the end of the campaigning season. Given the slow rate at which news was disseminated in the ancient world, news of the Persian defeat at Issus in November 333 may not have reached the fleet until after the end of the sailing season, so the Phoenician and Cypriot contingents were simply in no position to defect to Alexander until early April. By the time the Phoenician fleet arrived home, the siege of Tyre had been under way for two months. Alexander's military presence in Sidon would ensure that there would be no difficulty with his taking personal possession of the fleet.

Arrian gives us a quite detailed account of the numbers of ships Alexander acquired: the contingents of Aradus, Byblos and Sidon accounted for a total of about eighty Phoenician vessels. At around the same time he was joined by a detachment 'from Rhodes and nine other vessels, three from Soli and Mallus, ten from Lycia and a fifty-oared galley from Macedon'.[129] Soon after the news of the Persian defeat at Issus had reached Cyprus, the Cypriot kings also decided to join Alexander at Sidon: their fleet alone totalled some 120 ships. Arrian's total of 224 ships at Sidon generally agrees with Plutarch's figure of 200 and Curtius' claim that 190 ships took part in the surprise attack on Tyre.[130]

The acquisition of the Cypro-Phoenician fleet was undoubtedly the turning point in the siege of Tyre: before this Alexander had no effective fleet and therefore no real means of countering Tyrian naval action against him. This fleet assured that he could probe the outer defences of the city from all directions. This ability to attack from a number of positions and directions simultaneously was another hallmark strategy of Alexander. Even in his set-piece battles we can see his desire to have the Companion Cavalry attack the Persian centre from the right, at the same time as the heavy infantry was attacking from the front. Alexander realized the benefit of such tactics very early during his career and applied it to every possible situation. The ultimate breakthrough came when a group of hypaspists, operating as marines, penetrated the walls at the southern tip of the fortress, not as a direct result of the construction of the mole. The troops on the mole would have had the effect of diverting some of the defenders away from the southern section of the walls, as would the fleet that was operating around the whole perimeter of the besieged city.

Chapter 7

Siege Engines

—ᴍ—

Historical Developments

Catapults were probably first invented in the Greek world in 399, in Syracuse, under the patronage of Dionysius I. Diodorus tells us that in that year 'the entire city became one great arsenal'.[131] It seems that Dionysius gathered the finest engineers of the day from all over Sicily to construct for him vast quantities of the most modern pieces of military technology, as well as almost certainly to undertake research and development work into new forms of armaments. Diodorus goes on to say that:[132]

> Catapults were discovered at that time…a natural consequence of the assembly in one place of the most skilful craftsmen from all over the world.

A problem remains, however, as to what type of artillery Diodorus is describing: torsion or non-torsion catapults. There will be greater discussion on the technical differences later; for now it is sufficient to say that torsion engines were more complex and therefore probably a development from simpler non-torsion machines. In order for Diodorus to be describing the invention of torsion catapults we must be able to demonstrate the existence, before this date, of non-torsion engines, and we cannot. I think it highly unlikely that the technological jump could have occurred from bow and arrow to torsion catapults without an intervening step. Diodorus, therefore, must be describing the invention of non-torsion engines. It is inconceivable that non-torsion engines would have escaped the notice of Thucydides, if they had been in existence at the time of the Peloponnesian War. Thucydides presents the sieges of Plataea and Syracuse as showpieces, giving details on the most modern forms of attack and defence, including the use of a rather primitive, yet ingenious, form of flamethrower.[133] Catapults are not present.

In 414, in an interesting line in *The Birds*, Aristophanes has Euelpides say to Peisthetairos: 'You are already out-shooting Nicias with your machines'.[134] The word out-shooting can just as easily mean out-doing, and probably therefore refers to the construction of higher towers to allow slingers and archers to fire their projectiles over greater distances. This is, in all likelihood, little more than a military metaphor, and in the absence of more evidence we cannot use this line of Aristophanes as evidence of the existence of catapults at this time.

Diodorus also gives no indication that the Carthaginians possessed catapults in his descriptions of the sieges of Selinus and Himera in 409, or in his description of Acragas in 406.[135] We can probably infer, then, that catapults were not invented in the Greek world until 399, and that these catapults were of the non-torsion variety; but what of developments outside the Greek world?

There are two possible references in the Bible to the existence of catapults in the east. The first is in 2 Chronicles: 'Uzziah made in Jerusalem accurately designed machines to be on the towers and breastworks, to hurl missiles and large stones'.[136] This book of the Old Testament was written around 250, however, when siege technique was at a relatively high level, and the writer could easily be guilty of an anachronism. However, the biblical figure of Uzziah lived around the eighth century, making it even more unlikely that this passage represents a historical fact. These same objections cannot be used to disprove the second reference in Ezekiel, as that section was written around 580.[137] In this instance though, the Hebrew text uses the term 'battering ram', which was mistranslated into Greek as 'catapult', and so again there is no definitive evidence of the existence of catapults before 399.

Pliny provides us with some minor but interesting information that also must be addressed in his *Natural History*:[138]

> They say that Pisaeus invented hunting-spears and, among pieces of artillery, the scorpion; the Cretans invented the catapult, the Syro-Phoenicians the ballista and sling.

This evidence can again be dismissed as almost certainly a misunderstanding on the part of either Pliny or of his Hellenistic source resulting from the use of vague and anachronistic references.

There is one very interesting possible reference to the existence of catapults outside the Greek world long before 399, and from much farther east than Phoenicia. Sun Tzu, in his great work *The Art of War*, makes several references to 'machines'. He advises to a general 'keep your machines in good repair', a little later advising that, before undertaking a siege, he should 'take three months to prepare your machines and three months to complete your siege engineering'.

He then goes on to say that he 'means that it is necessary to take time to really prepare machines and constructions thoroughly'. Sun Tzu then strongly advises the general not to lose patience, but to 'wait for the siege machines' to arrive before beginning to assault a fortified position.[139] Sun Tzu strongly advocated the bloodless victory, repeatedly saying that the most skilled commanders were those who could defeat their enemies without fighting. We can probably conclude therefore that Sun Tzu was not describing catapults but some other, unspecified but less advanced pieces of technology, possibly some form of rams, ladders and screens for instance. Diodorus is, therefore, in all probability describing the first appearance in the world of artillery, created in Syracuse in 399 under the auspices of Dionysius I.

It is unclear how quickly non-torsion catapults spread to mainland Greece, but a significant turning point occurred in 354 BC, when Philip was beginning to become involved in the affairs of Thessaly. He met, and was defeated by, Onomarchus of Phocis in a brilliant piece of strategy where Onomarchus lured the Macedonians into a horse-shoe shaped canyon where they could use catapults stationed out of reach on the cliff-tops of the canyon walls. It seems unlikely that the Macedonians possessed artillery before this point because this incident had a significant impact on Philip, prompting him to instruct his engineers to construct siege engines and no doubt to attempt to improve on the current design. Developments in Macedon were apparently slow, as the Macedonian siege train had had little impact until the siege of Perinthus in 340, some fourteen years later. Even by this time Diodorus only records arrow-shooting catapults as being in the possession of Philip. Arrian adds to this the key point that 'Macedonian stone-throwers do not appear until Alexander's attack on Halicarnassus some years later'.[140]

Early non-torsion engines were, in all honesty, of limited value; they were not powerful enough to destroy walls by themselves and they of course had very limited range. Their range was probably only around 180-

230m for the earliest models. Improvements in design, therefore, were imperative and, as E W Marsden concluded:[141]

> although definite information simply does not exist, a good deal of circumstantial evidence suggests that the principle of torsion was first discovered in Macedon under the auspices of Philip II.

The discovery of this principle was a watershed in siege warfare as it allowed projectiles to be fired with greater propulsive force over a longer distance. Arrian 4.30 gives us an excellent picture of the potential of this new invention from the northeastern frontier: the bridge constructed over the ravine during the assault on Aornus took three days to complete, with Alexander's stone-throwers attacking the enemy after the first day's work. In the first day the bridge was extended 180m; we can therefore assume that the ravine was 550m wide and that Alexander's torsion engines could fire around 365m. Torsion engines are first mentioned during the siege of Perinthus, although these were arrow-throwers and were only used to assault troops on the walls, rather than the walls themselves. This breakthrough was turned into a significant advantage for the attacking side when Alexander's engineers applied this principle to stone-throwing machines. With the creation of the first recorded stone-throwing catapults, Alexander had the ability to assault city walls from a distance for the first time in history.

Siege equipment had existed in both Greece and the Near East for a considerable length of time before the career of Alexander, but it was, by the standards of the fourth century, rather primitive. The attackers could not assault the walls from a distance and were forced to use rams and scaling ladders, both of which would have resulted in large numbers of casualties among the attackers.[142] A circumvallation of earth could be used, as at Plataea in 429, as a means of elevating the troops to somewhere close to the top of the city's walls. This was also a tactic used by Alexander during the siege of Gaza, but here he mounted his siege engines upon the top of the mound of earth: towers were also used to achieve the same result. Before the invention of the catapult, however, there were only two real ways of capturing a fortified position: starvation or betrayal. If a city could be completely cut off it could be starved into submission, but this was often time consuming and did not guarantee success. We also have to take into account that Greece was a world where there were very distinct campaigning seasons; commanders often could not afford the time to starve a city. The best hope for an attacking general was to have the city betrayed to him from within, either by a faction of supporters or by the promise of gold as a reward. This is an area where Philip excelled: it was once said that Philip could capture any city as long as he could get a mule laden with gold to the gates. Before the widespread use of catapults, and particularly torsion stone-throwers, the advantage in siege warfare always lay with the defenders.

Knowledge of catapults seems to have taken some time to spread to other parts of the Greek world after its invention in Sicily. The first city-states on the mainland to obtain the new weapon were probably Sparta and Athens. Plutarch records Archidamus' reaction to witnessing a demonstration of a catapult around 370: 'Heracles, man's martial valour is of no avail any more'.[143] This is an extremely interesting passage as it illustrates that the effect on morale was far greater than its actual military impact at this time. A fragmentary inscription from Athens that details stockpiled items on the acropolis in 371/0 lists two boxes of catapult bolts, and since it is unlikely that the Athenians would have stockpiled catapult bolts without the necessary catapult, we can infer that the Athenians possessed them by at least this date.

The spread of catapults to the rest of Greece probably came from direct contact with one or both of the two great city-states. The Phocians, for instance, were on friendly terms with both Athens and Sparta at the outbreak of the Sacred War, and the weapons that Onomarchus used to defeat Philip probably originated in either Athens or Sparta. Their use did not spread throughout the Greek world: when Philip besieged Perinthus, a relatively important state, there is no indication that the defenders possessed artillery of any kind.

Technical Details

It is usual to divide ancient artillery pieces into two broad categories according to the means by which the propulsive force is applied to the projectile, these being the torsion and non-torsion engines. In a non-torsion engine, surely the first of the two classes to be invented, the propulsive force is supplied by a compound bow similar to, but stronger than, the standard bow of the day, whereas in a torsion engine the force is supplied by a spring of sinew, hair or some other resilient material. Of the five surviving ancient sources only Heron gives details on the earliest form of both torsion and non-torsion engines. The so-called '*gastraphetes*' ('belly-bow') was the first non-torsion engine. Heron was writing in Alexandria in the first century AD, but used Ctesibius, the third century BC writer, as his main source, and so his work is effectively third century. The engine owed its name to the fact that the operator had to rest the end of the machine on his stomach while physically pulling the bowstring into place, although later models were fitted with a winch allowing the bowstring to be drawn back further, adding to the effective range of the weapon.

The *gastraphetes* was constructed and transported in three sections: the bow, and the base, which itself was in two pieces. This 'flat pack' construction added to the difficulty in deploying the weapon in the field. The construction materials used in the actual bow are the subject of some debate, but if it was a compound bow then it would consist of a central core of wood with a layer of horn glued to the inside of the bow, and a layer of sinew being attached to the outer side. The horn was there to resist compression and provide propulsive force by trying to return to its original position, and the sinew would resist expansion, again supplying force to the projectile.

The bolts that were fired from the *gastraphetes* were essentially large arrows, although it appears to have taken a process of experimentation in order to determine the optimum size and weight distribution for these bolts. Diodorus tells us that 'catapult bolts of all kinds were prepared'.[144] This could of course imply different types of catapults being constructed, but I think it more likely that this was simply a trial and error process to determine the optimum bolt design for the *gastraphetes*.

The *gastraphetes* was a significant invention, but the compound bow was limited as to the force that it could apply to a projectile, meaning that it could not be used to attack walls directly. It was with this in mind that Heron reports that the Syracusans:[145]

wished to increase both the size of the missile and the force of projection. They sought to make the arms of the bow more powerful, but they could not realise their intention by the use of composite bows.

In order to increase the propulsive force of the machine, the Macedonians first investigated the properties of the three resilient materials used in the composite bow: sinew, wood and horn. The principle of torsion was probably developed because they wished to isolate the sinew which, they believed, contributed the major force in composite bows.

The realization that sinew on its own gave greater propulsive force led to a redesigning of the engine itself. The first torsion engines were similar in design to the non-torsion engines of the day, except that the compound bow was replaced by two separate wooden struts:[146]

> around each of which they wrapped strand after strand and layer after layer of sinew cord. The two resulting bundles of sinew, each with its own frame, formed the new springs.

This new design also incorporated a certain amount of extra wood in the framework of the device to cope with the extra stress that the machine would be subject to, especially at the front end where the two struts were attached to the frame.

Another innovation, seemingly datable to the reign of Alexander, is the use of ship-mounted artillery. This strategy allowed the besieger of a maritime city, Tyre being the perfect example, not only to block off the harbour but, more importantly, to force the defenders to divide their troops along the city's defensive perimeter. This had the effect of not allowing them to concentrate on any given sector. This essentially allowed Alexander to conduct an outflanking attack, which was in many ways his trademark.

Arrian does not give us precise details as to what these ship-mounted machines actually were, but one particular passage does seem to imply an answer. The engines themselves, which were mounted on transport vessels, could not approach within effective range because there were a large number of rocks in the water close to Tyre, the rocks having been placed there by the defenders precisely to prevent a ship-borne assault by the Macedonians. The crews of the ships decided to drag these rocks onboard; two possible explanations for what happened next are feasible. The rocks were either transported out to sea and dropped into deeper water, or they were fired out to sea from the artillery pieces on the ships. Arrian's use of the word *aphiesan* seems to provide the answer: it implies a throwing motion rather than simply dropping, and therefore we can assume that the artillery pieces Alexander had mounted upon his ships were indeed stone-throwing engines. Given the fact that the stones in the sea were formerly part of the walls and had been dropped there by the defenders to prevent the close approach of Alexander's fleet, we can make an estimation of the size of the stone sections that made up the defensive walls in that sector of the city. We know that the maximum weight a stone throwing catapult could handle was three talents (perhaps 75kg), and we further know that Alexander's ship-borne artillery were specially designed by Archidemus so they were capable of firing larger pieces. As a consequence, the rocks that made up the walls of Tyre in that area can not have been much heavier than three or four talents – which is surprisingly small.

As mentioned above, siege towers were not a new invention, but those used by Alexander do seem to have been of exceptional size. A description of a giant siege tower, designed for Alexander by his engineer Posidonius, can be found in Biton. Alexander's towers were constructed and transported in sections for easy assembly on site. They were also wheeled for freedom of movement (the wheels sank into the sand at Gaza, causing considerable damage to the flooring of the towers and injuries to the troops inside).[147] Furthermore, they were equipped with drawbridges in order that the attackers could reach the walls: towers must always be greater than the height of the walls they are attacking or they are useless.

Artillery in Field Campaigns

When considering the uses of ancient artillery in field campaigns we should resist any temptation to draw parallels with modern artillery pieces. Modern artillery is often located several kilometres behind the front and can cause considerable damage to the enemy's positions by concentrating fire: a brief artillery bombardment before an assault was one of the fundamental principles of *Blitzkrieg*. Ancient artillery was very different: it had limited range, probably not much more than 365m, and before around 100 AD no artillery pieces were mounted permanently on mobile carriages. This meant that individual pieces had to be transported to the area in which they would be used, unloaded, assembled and then fired. This serious lack of mobility also meant that the sighting of artillery pieces in field operations was of prime importance: they had to be located where the enemy was unlikely or unable to overrun them.

By Alexander's day, artillery was able to perform two roles: destruction and suppression. The discovery of the principle of torsion allowed a besieger to assault the walls of a city directly from a distance; this was an ability that had not existed before. Artillery also performed the vital role of suppression, both during sieges, when it was used to clear the walls of defenders, and during field operations, when it could prevent the enemy from attacking until you were ready, such as at the Jaxartes (see later).

The first recorded incident of artillery being used in a field campaign occurs towards the beginning of the reign of Philip, when he was first becoming interested in the affairs of Thessaly.[148] Onomarchus, the Phocian general, had taken up a position in a semi-circular range of hills, his artillery being positioned on the ridge above. When Philip attacked, Onomarchus feigned flight and the Macedonians gave chase. At the key moment, the Phocians reformed, and at the same time the catapults rained down a devastating hail upon the disorganized Macedonian infantry, forcing them to withdraw. It was probably the surprise and the panic that it caused, rather than the actual effectiveness of the artillery fire, which was so devastating to the Macedonians at this time. If there is one incident that caused Philip to invest so much energy in developing an artillery arm, it was certainly this one.

Despite all of the many battles and campaigns fought by Alexander, there are only two instances where he deployed artillery pieces in a field operation, both of which were in rather special circumstances. The first occurred when he had been compelled to abandon the siege of Pellium in 335 and was in the process of withdrawing his troops to a safer area. Safety was only available once across the ford of the river Eordaicus. Most of his troops managed to cross safely, but his rearguard, consisting of the Agrianians and some archers, had considerable difficulty in disengaging from the enemy. Arrian reports:[149]

> He deployed his artillery on the bank of the river and ordered his men to shoot, at maximum range, all the types of missile that are hurled from machines. He also ordered the archers, who had already plunged in, to shoot from mid-stream. Glaucias' men did not dare to advance within range. Meanwhile the Macedonians crossed the river safely, so that not one casualty was suffered in the withdrawal.

The second incident of Alexander's employment of catapults occurred during his crossing of the Jaxartes River in 329. A group of Scythians was occupying the far bank, making any attempt at crossing extremely hazardous. Arrian records the events that followed:[150]

> When all the skin floats were ready and the army in full equipment drawn up on the river bank, the catapults, at the word of command, opened up on the Scythians who were riding along the edge of the water on the further side. Some of them were hit; one was pierced through both shield and breastplate and fell dead from his horse. The Scythians were taken completely aback by the long range of the catapults, and that, together with the loss of a good man, induced them to withdraw a short distance from the river, whereupon Alexander, seeing their consternation, ordered the trumpets to sound and himself led the way over the water, followed by his men.

Curtius records that Alexander's catapults were mounted on boats in midstream.[151] This is possible, although there is a good chance that Curtius is confusing contemporary Imperial Roman practice in the crossing of wide rivers under opposition.

All three of these examples of the use of artillery in the field illustrate very well the limited theatre in which they could be employed. They had to be close enough to the enemy in order for their projectiles to reach; they also had to be on ground that was easily defensible, or did not require defending at all. These three examples, and particularly the latter two, show very clearly that the psychological effect of the weapons was out of all proportion to their actual effectiveness. On the two occasions when Alexander employed catapults only one man is recorded as being killed, yet they helped in ensuring a successful outcome to both operations. Their true usefulness in field operations lay in their shock value, and in the confusion that they caused amongst the enemy. Many of Alexander's opponents, particularly the Scythians, may never have seen such a weapon. These native troops may well have been prepared to die in hand-to-hand combat, but they were evidently not so prepared to risk their lives when there was no possibility of striking back at the enemy.

Chapter 8

Command Structure

—꿈—

The command structure of the Macedonian army was extremely complex, consisting of many separate layers of authority. At the highest levels it is quite well known; the same cannot be said of lesser ranks, but there are hints that suggest that, even at its lowest levels, it was as complex as the more powerful positions. As with many areas of Alexander's empire, and particularly within the army, the command structure was continually evolving as new positions were created and others became obsolete. The most significant changes, however, were probably politically motivated. Alexander gradually changed the army from being that of Philip, through the influence of Parmenio and his family, to being his own, particularly after 331/0, when Parmenio's influence had been removed.

Macedonian Heavy Infantry

At its lowest levels the command structure of the heavy infantry can be deduced from its gradations of pay. The smallest tactical unit of the heavy infantry was the *dekas* or 'file'. As the name implies the *dekas* had once consisted of ten men, but at some point long before the reign of Alexander it had been expanded to sixteen. Of these sixteen men, twelve were rank and file with the other four being of superior status. Of these four, one was the *dekadarch* or file leader, one was a *dimoirites* or half-file leader and the other two were *dekastateroi* or half-file closers. Arrian tells us that the *dekastateroi* were paid the equivalent of one and a half the pay of a rank-and-file soldier, around forty-five drachmas a month. The *dimoirites* received double pay of around sixty drachmas a month.[152] Bosworth seems to have made a slight error in interpreting this passage in Arrian, claiming that there were two *dimoiritai* and only one *dekastateros*, but Arrian's text seems quite clear on this point.[153]

Thirty-two *decades* formed a *lochos,* consisting of 512 men and being commanded by a *lochagos.* Three *lochoi* formed a *taxis,* which was the fundamental unit of the Macedonian heavy infantry, commanded by a *taxiarch.* Each *taxis* therefore consisted of 1,540 men, of whom 1,152 were rank and file and in receipt of the basic one drachma a day. Initially Alexander crossed the Hellespont with six *taxeis,* later expanded to seven around the time of the invasion of India. Therefore the command structure for a typical *taxis* of heavy infantry was:

- *Taxiarch*
- *Lochagos* (x3)
- *Dekadarch* (x96)
- *Dimoirites* (x96)
- *Dekastateros* (x192)
- *Rank and File* (x1,152)

The manpower indicated is, of course, paper strength, assuming that each *taxis* was at full strength. The six *taxiarchs* appear to have all been of the same rank with none holding superiority. Indeed there was no overall commander of the heavy infantry (excluding the one possible reference in Arrian discussed earlier) as there was for, say, the Companion Cavalry. This is because there really was no such organization as the 'Macedonian phalanx', the *taxeis* themselves frequently being used as separate tactical units, or in groups of two or three (see Chapter 1). This development came largely after 331 when the army entered northeastern Iran and smaller, more mobile forces were required.

Arrian makes a seemingly strange claim that:[154]

On the right wing of the attacking force Alexander had the guards' division under his personal command. In touch with them were the infantry battalions, forming the whole centre of the line and commanded by the various officers whose turn of duty happened to fall upon that day.

This is almost certainly evidence of a rotational system within the phalanx. It could be a reference to the order in which the *taxeis* appeared each day, and we are explicitly told in the sources that that the actual order of each *taxis* did rotate each day, or it could be that the minor commands within a *taxis* were rotated to give junior commanders more experience of slightly different roles.[155]

The Macedonian heavy infantry appear to have undergone very few serious changes in the command structure over the course of the campaign. The huge numbers of reinforcements received between the great set-piece battles of Issus and Gaugamela seem to have been incorporated within the existing *taxeis*, presumably adding to the numbers of rank and file rather than to the officer corps. The first evidence for a seventh *taxis* does not appear until the time of the invasion of India, where Arrian names seven *taxiarchs* operating simultaneously.[156]

Hypaspists

At the time of the invasion of Persia, another of Parmenio's sons, Nicanor, was the commander of the hypaspists. The hypaspists were the elite formation of the Macedonian heavy infantry and their tactical and strategic roles were many and varied. The hypaspists were organized into three *chiliarchies* of 1,000 men, each commanded by a *chiliarch*. This is true after 331 at least: before 331 it is uncertain (see Chapter 2). One of these *chiliarchies* was designated the *agema*, perhaps commanded by Alexander himself, or more likely by an unknown individual, as Alexander was usually with the Companion Cavalry during set-piece battles. The *chiliarchs* themselves were of markedly lower status than the *taxiarchs* of the heavy infantry, being more like a *lochagos*. This is at first sight rather surprising, considering that the hypaspists were the elite units of the heavy infantry, receiving only the very best of the new recruits into their ranks. We should remember, however, that, unlike the heavy infantry, the hypaspists had an overall commander, Nicanor, who was at a significant level within the command structure, ensuring that their status was considerably higher than that of an infantry *taxis*.

As with the rest of the army, the command structure of the hypaspists was significantly changed at the end of 331. The *chiliarchies* were subdivided into two new units, *pentakosiarchies*, thus adding an entirely new layer into the command structure, albeit a very lowly one.[157] These new officers were again appointed by Alexander on the basis of merit rather than seniority, and again owed their allegiance to the king himself. We saw earlier how important this innovation was to the king, particularly later in his career as he became ever more paranoid.

Companion Cavalry

The numbers of the Companion Cavalry are not certain, although Diodorus gives the figure of 1,800 and most now accept the figure of 1,800 as at least being very close to the actual figure. We do know that by 333 the Companion Cavalry consisted of eight *ilai* (squadrons) of 200 men, each commanded by an *ilarch*. We have no information of from the beginning of his reign, but we do know that along with the general reorganization of the army in 331 an *ile* was further divided into smaller units. Arrian tells us 'He also – this was an innovation – formed two *lochoi* (companies) in each cavalry squadron'.[158]

Curtius hints at a reorganization, and confirms that commanders would from this time be promoted on the basis of ability and not of regional affiliations. However he does not mention the division of *ile*, preferring to concentrate on the hypaspists. From 331 the subdivision of *ile* was into two *hekatostyes* of 100 men; there is evidence that each *ile* was again subdivided into *tetrarchia*, of which there would have been four per *ile*. The *tetrarchia* is only recorded once in Arrian, at the turning of the Persian Gates in January 330, not before or after, but the unit was small enough that this is not surprising as they would mostly have operated in the larger units.[159]

One of the *ilai* was given the title *ile basilike*, also frequently called the *agema*, or royal squadron: this unit was also of higher status than the rest. The royal squadron was of double strength and was charged with defending the king when he fought on horseback; they were his personal bodyguard in all of the set-piece battles. The overall command of the Companion Cavalry was in the hands of Philotas - until his execution in October 330, that is.

The *ilarchs* seem to have been relatively minor in rank, probably on a par with an infantry *lochagos*. *Ilarchs* are seldom mentioned by name in any of the sources and are never given separate commands of their own. The only one that achieved any level of distinction was Cleitus the Black, the commander of the royal squadron.

After the execution of Philotas in 330, the entire Macedonian cavalry was reorganized *en masse*. The basic tactical formation was now not the *ile* but the 'hipparchy'. These new units are first recorded by Arrian during 329. *Ilai* do still appear in the sources but they become sub-divisions of a hipparchy, each hipparchy comprising a minimum of two *ilai* and thus 400 men. The *ilai* were also sub-divided into two lochoi, the commanders of whom were given the title *lochagos*, as with the commander of an infantry unit. Alexander appointed these commanders personally on a basis of merit rather than superiority, thus breaking with tradition. This was a policy that was entirely consistent with Alexander making the army loyal to him alone. This began to occur some time during 331 BC, probably after Gaugamela, when the last great batch of reinforcements arrived from Macedon. This was the beginning of the policy, that I have noted a number of times, of reducing the army's ties of loyalty to its individual commanders, ultimately making them loyal to Alexander alone. Thus a new layer of sub-commanders was added in the command structure of the army, one which owed its loyalty directly to Alexander, to some extent breaking the link between the troops and their commanders. There are two possible reasons for this change. Perhaps Alexander came to the conclusion that the *ilai* were simply too small, at 200 men, to cope with the different style of fighting in the entirely different theatre that was to be their next challenge. The army would no longer be fighting set-piece battles, but would require far more mobility and flexibility as it moved into the northeast of Iran The second possible explanation was a desire on the part of Alexander to increase the relative superiority of the Companion Cavalry over the heavy infantry, each hipparch now being of a higher status than a *lochagos* (see Chapter 3).

The term '*ile basilike*' also disappeared at this time and was replaced by the term *agema*, the nomenclature becoming the same as for the hypaspists. The actual number of cavalry hipparchies is unknown, but it is assumed that there were eight during the Indian campaign. The position left vacant by the death of Philotas was not directly filled. He was instead replaced by two men: Alexander's life-long friend Hephaestion and Cleitus the Black. Both men were effectively of equal status within the command structure. Arrian gives the reason for this step as that 'he [Alexander] did not think it advisable that one man – even a personal friend – should have control of so large a body of cavalry'.[160]

Allies and Mercenaries

The Thessalian cavalry were without doubt the most important contingent of this aspect of the army. They were probably equal in number to the Companion Cavalry and very close to them in terms of quality. Overall command of this vitally-important unit was given to Alexander's second-in-command, Parmenio. The command structure of the Thessalian cavalry was very similar to that of the Companions, being divided into *ilai*. They were not, however, allowed their own national commanders, but a senior Macedonian officer was appointed to command each unit. The Thessalian cavalry also had a unit which performed the same role as the royal squadron of the Companions; this was known as the 'Pharsalian contingent'.

The other allied cavalry contingents, although considerably less important, were again organized along similar lines, being divided into *ilai* and each having a Macedonian commander. The appointment of a Macedonian commander at the head of non-Macedonian troops, be they cavalry or infantry, was the general policy of Alexander throughout his reign. Even the mercenary contingents were treated in exactly this same fashion, Menander being their overall commander. These Macedonian officers, however, were relatively unimportant in the overall command structure and few achieved any kind of distinction.

The fleets that accompanied the army of invasion were almost exclusively non-Macedonian, being provided by the member states of the League of Corinth. Each ship was captained by a native of the contributing city, and where a city-state provided more than one ship, they also supplied a 'commodore' for their particular contingent. As with other non-Macedonian units however, overall command of the fleet was with a Macedonian officer.

Bodyguard

The term 'bodyguard' is quite a confusing one, as there appear to be two entirely separate groups within the army that carry this title. The first is an apparently-quite-strong detachment of heavy infantry. Arrian, three times, tells us that Alexander took with him the bodyguards *and* some of the hypaspists; this would seem to strongly suggest that they were not simply a detachment of the hypaspists, who were themselves often called 'the guards'.[161] Diodorus tells us that at the Battle of Gaugamela, Hephaestion 'had commanded the bodyguards'.[162] This passage again strongly suggests that we are not here talking about a detachment of the hypaspists, as at this time Nicanor was still their commander and only died later that same year. The bodyguards seem to have been a relatively minor force, perhaps of the order of a couple of hundred strong. The relative position of their commander within the overall command structure of the army is unknown; the only commander named is Hephaestion at Gaugamela, who was of course a very senior figure. Hephaestion's seniority probably had more to do with his closeness to Alexander than the importance of the bodyguards as a military force: his successor after Gaugamela is never mentioned, for instance. This group could well represent a carry-over from a much older organization that pre-dated Philip's reforms.

The group that most interests us here are the *somatophylakes basilikoi*, or 'royal bodyguard', originally seven strong, this number being rigidly maintained. The number was probably connected to their historical function of guarding the king's tent. They were increased to eight in India, however, when Peucestas was promoted to this rank as a sign of gratitude by Alexander for saving his life during the attack on the capital city of the Malli.

The bodyguards occupied a position within the command structure that is difficult to define. The group as a whole formed part of Alexander's immediate entourage, and seem certain to have been among his closest friends and most-trusted advisors. Membership of the bodyguard was obviously incompatible with any post that involved their being away from court for any length of time: both Balacrus and Menes were replaced as soon as they were assigned to the command of provinces.[163] For reasons that seem less clear, inclusion within the bodyguard was also incompatible with a command within the army. Before Gaugamela, there is no recorded instance of a member of the bodyguard simultaneously holding a senior command. Bodyguards are occasionally reported briefly holding minor commands, such as Ptolemy, who commanded a joint force of hypaspists and light infantry during the siege of Halicarnassus, but this was rare.[164] If any bodyguard were promoted to a senior command, he would immediately lose his title and be replaced. This happened, for instance, when Ptolemy became a *taxiarch* (this was not the famous historian and son of Lagos, but another very obscure individual: Ptolemy was a very common name in Macedonia). As a group they probably enjoyed the same status as a *taxiarch*, but did not, as such, occupy any position within the command structure. They were, however, still influential as they were among the king's closest advisors.

This rather rigid system which applied to the bodyguard, as with almost everything else in the army, evolved considerably over time. After the death of Parmenio we hear of instances of bodyguards receiving senior, albeit temporary, commands. In 328, for instance, Alexander left four *taxeis* of heavy infantry in Bactria, along with their commanders. The remainder of the army was then divided into five columns, three of which were commanded by known bodyguards.[165] The deaths of Parmenio and Philotas represent something of a watershed in Alexander's career, as will be discussed below.

Evolution of the Command Structure

One of the major changes that occurred in the command structure over the course of Alexander's reign was that the cavalry commands became increasingly important, relative to their previously-equivalent infantry commands. By the time of the death of Philotas Alexander was becoming increasingly disinclined to place such large numbers of men under a single commander; with this in mind he divided the command of the Companion cavalry between Hephaestion and Cleitus the Black. Individual hipparchs also became increasingly important in their own right, becoming roughly equal in status to the position of an infantry *taxiarch*. At the beginning of the invasion of India, the commanders of the heavy infantry who were most highly favoured by Alexander were promoted to command hipparchies of Companion Cavalry; namely Perdiccas, Craterus and Cleitus the White. This again illustrated that moving from an infantry command to that of cavalry was considered a promotion.

During this process, the royal bodyguard evolved into an important position within the command structure. Perdiccas was promoted to a hipparchy, from a *taxis* of heavy infantry, in 327; by 330 he also had the title of bodyguard. This was a dual function which was also enjoyed by Alexander's favourite, Hephaestion. The Peithon who was a bodyguard by 325 is very probably the same Peithon who is attested as a *taxiarch* in 326/5.[166] An infantry command was rare, however; members of the bodyguard were usually given commands within the Companion Cavalry, in alignment with its increasing importance. This desire on the part of Alexander to systematically downgrade the relative importance of the heavy infantry can perhaps be attributed to the fact that Alexander saw them as a potential, and increasing, problem. It was from the ranks of the infantry that the mutinies at the Hyphasis and Opis had come, and it would not be surprising if Alexander had deliberately aimed at increasing the prestige and importance of the cavalry relative to the infantry. This would have been to re-establish the situation that had existed before his reign, where the cavalry were clearly the units of greatest prestige. It is also likely that the heavy infantry had become less prestigious, simply because the army was engaged in northeastern Iran at this time and they were not as heavily involved in the fighting as they had been during earlier campaigns.

From 330, when Alexander entered the northeast of the former Persian Empire, he was faced with an entirely new situation: that of guerrilla warfare. This led to a willingness on the part of Alexander to divide his force, seemingly indiscriminately, between various commanders. Before this time if a second column was required it would consist of allied and mercenary troops, the Macedonians almost always staying with the king. As mentioned above, in 328 Alexander left four *taxeis* of Macedonian heavy infantry in Bactria and divided the rest of the army into five groups. These new commands were given to a fairly select group of Alexander's closest friends: Craterus, Hephaestion, Coenus and Perdiccas were usually the first choices, with Ptolemy, Leonnatus and Peithon used where more columns were employed. When Alexander entered India, Hephaestion and Perdiccas were sent ahead to the Indus with a large force comprising around half of the Macedonians and all of the mercenary infantry.

One of the most important features of the changes in the command structure of the Macedonian army towards the end of Alexander's reign was the increasing mobility of commands. Individual generals still kept their titles, but were expected to command entirely separate units as situations presented themselves. For example, in 327 three *taxiarchs*, Meleager, Attalus and Gorgias, were detached from their *taxeis* and were given the commands of a group of mercenary cavalry and infantry. They were then employed on diversionary movements along the river banks. Another example is that of Coenus, a *taxiarch* since 334, who was employed as a cavalry commander at the Hydaspes.[167]

This move towards an increasing mobility of command was for two main reasons, the first being military. As Alexander entered the next phase of the campaign after 331, he increasingly met with an enemy that operated on significantly different lines from that faced early in the campaign. He was also faced with fighting in a new theatre and in different conditions, all of which required the army to be considerably more flexible than it had previously been.

There is surely a second, and in my opinion significantly more important factor at work here: namely politics. Alexander seems to have been becoming increasingly concerned about assigning large bodies of troops to a single commander indefinitely: there was for instance probably no overall commander of the heavy infantry, and the positions vacated by Parmenio and Philotas were never filled, the Companion Cavalry receiving co-commanders. Alexander increasingly detached individuals from their commands and gave them different assignments. He also employed new layers in the command structure and made promotions according to merit. These changes had a two-fold effect: the commanders became loyal primarily to him, since they owed their positions directly to the king's favour; secondly, the focus of the army's loyalty was also the king, as their commanders often changed and their territorial origins slowly eroded. Alexander made himself the sole focus of every individual, whatever his rank, within the army.

The Price of Parmenio's Support

Parmenio was probably the single most important political figure in Macedonia, apart from the king, during the reign of Philip; this is true of the early part of Alexander's reign too. He, as well as various of his family members, was well entrenched at court and seems to have had political connections with both factions contending for the succession in the last years of Philip's reign. Thus when Philip was assassinated, Parmenio was in a prime position to act as king-maker. He was in a position to offer the support of most of the lowland barons; this would leave Amyntas or any other potential rival with only the possibility of forming a coalition of the fringes of Macedonia and rebellious Greek cities. Parmenio was evidently a skilled political operator and knew well the strength of his position; Alexander was forced to pay a heavy price for Parmenio's support, but in 336 he was in no position to argue. When the Macedonian army crossed the Hellespont into Asia almost every key command was held by one of Parmenio's sons, brothers, or some other kinsman. We have already noted that two of Parmenio's sons were commanders of the hypaspists (Nicanor) and the Companion Cavalry (Philotas), with Parmenio himself commanding the Thessalian cavalry and essentially being second in command of the whole army. Parmenio's brother, Asander, probably commanded the light cavalry, and certainly received the satrapy of Sardis as soon as it was conquered. Parmenio's supporters were also firmly entrenched in positions of power, men like the four sons of Andromenes and the brothers Coenus and Cleander. Many of the commanders of the army of invasion were little younger than Parmenio himself: when Justin tells us that headquarters looked 'more like the senate of some old-time republic' he is probably not exaggerating in his description, although it is a far from flattering one.[168]

The Macedonian army down to 330 was at its very core Philip's; they were his veterans and his commanders. Philip's influence was always present, and frequently felt by Alexander in the form of Parmenio. This was a situation which Alexander could not tolerate indefinitely. He allowed the command structure to remain relatively unchanged whilst his success was still in the balance, but after Gaugamela Alexander began to make serious and sweeping changes to the army, changes which were made considerably easier by the assassinations of both Philotas and Parmenio. Some authorities have argued that Alexander was plotting for the best part of six years to remove Parmenio's grip on the army, and see the final execution of Parmenio and Philotas as being the culmination of this plotting; this seems unlikely to be true. Why would he, for example, have left Parmenio in Ecbatana with a considerable part of the army and his treasury if he did not trust his loyalty, or if he was about to act against him? Alexander, on the whole, seems to have been more impulsive and spontaneous than this theory would give him credit for: it is more likely that Alexander seized his opportunity without having engineered it. Alexander was gambling that the army loved him more than they loved the old general, and he was right. Although the Thessalian cavalry perhaps did not take it well, they were not a significant part of the army after this, and indeed were disbanded entirely soon after. Following the death of Parmenio, Alexander would never again allow large bodies of troops to be commanded by any one individual for any length of time. Dissention was met with ruthlessness; the army had at last become his and his alone.

Chapter 9

The Army in Action

—∽—

Alexander's conquests remain some of the most impressive in the whole of the annals of military history. By his actions, and those of his army, he has gained a measure of immortality that few ever achieve. This book has been an examination of Alexander's army, its composition and structure, but it would not be complete without a discussion of Alexander's campaigns. We have seen the tools that enabled Alexander to achieve empire, but we must come to understand how the Macedonian was able to conquer the largest, richest and most powerful empire the western world had yet seen; and do it in a matter of only three or four years. This dating assumes that the Persian Empire was defeated with the Battle of Gaugamela in 331, some resistance did still remain after this point, notably in the northeast of the former empire.

Alexander's campaigns were many and various, encompassing mountain warfare, minor skirmishes, massive set-piece battles, great sieges and guerrilla actions. In a very short career, Alexander experienced every form of warfare that the ancient world had to offer (although his naval experience was limited to the siege of Tyre), and adapted his tactics brilliantly every time he was presented with a new challenge. We saw above that he even went to the extent of completely reorganizing the army to adapt to the new challenges of the northeastern satrapies. Given the scope of Alexander's battles, there is not the space here to examine each individually, only to look at three of his seminal campaigns: the Balkans, Issus and Tyre. Within these three campaigns we see Alexander at his most brilliant; we also see the depths of the training, discipline and talent possessed by the army and some of its key components.

The Balkans

Alexander's first campaign in the Balkans offers us some fascinating insights into the evolution of some key strategies that were to be continually developed throughout his career. The early campaigns are only recorded in any depth by Arrian: Strabo and Diodorus, for example, offer little that can be added.[169]

The assassination of Philip II had been followed by general unrest on Macedonia's northern border, and in the spring of 335 he set off north, into the Balkans to quell an uprising.[170] The campaign was against the 'Triballi and Illyrians': the Triballi occupied the plain to the south of the Danube, in what was later to become the Roman province of Moesia; they probably also extended some way to the east towards the Black Sea. The location of the Illyrians is a little more difficult to determine; the name is probably used by Arrian in a general sense to refer to those tribes to the northwest of Macedonia.[171]

Mount Haemus

The first stage of the Balkan campaign saw Alexander set off for the territory of the free Thracians, with the ultimate aim of crossing the Haemus range. The Thracians opposed his crossing by occupying a pass, although exactly which pass is in doubt. The incident in the pass was, in reality, an extremely minor affair, but is worthy of inclusion because of Alexander's response to a unique problem. The Thracians had taken up a defensive position in the pass, with the intention of using their wagons as a defensive palisade, or of sending them crashing down upon the advancing Macedonians.[172] Arrian leaves us in no doubt that the wagons were used as projectiles, but exactly how is far less clear. He constantly refers to them in the plural; is this intended to mean that several were sent down simultaneously, side by side as it were, or should it be taken to mean one after the other? The presumed narrowness of the pass would tend to preclude the former, and therefore we should accept that several wagons were sent down the slope consecutively against the Macedonians.[173]

Alexander's counter-measures are the most interesting part of this encounter. Arrian tells us that he instructed those of his troops who were able to break ranks and allow the carts to pass through: this is exactly the strategy that would be later used so successfully against Darius' scythed chariots at Gaugamela. Where space prevented this they were to lie prone and cover their bodies with interlocking shields.[174] How was this to be achieved with only the small *pelte* for protection? I noted earlier that the Macedonian heavy infantry were sufficiently well trained to be able to employ a range of weapons. On occasions such as this it is possible that the heavy infantry were equipped as regular hoplites. There is no evidence that Philip or Alexander ever ordered the production of large numbers of hoplite panoplies for the heavy infantry, as the expense alone would have been prohibitive. It is possible that hoplite shields could have been temporarily commandeered from the more heavily armoured of the allies and mercenaries. Thousands of panoplies would not have been required as not all of the heavy infantry would have been able to operate in such a limited space. The brilliance of this stratagem is demonstrated by the fact that no fatalities are recorded on the Macedonian side for this skirmish. We can see here Alexander developing and implementing an entirely novel approach to a unique problem; we can also see that the infantry had the training and discipline required to perform their task admirably.

Peuce Island

Once Alexander had crossed the Haemus range, he continued in a northerly direction into territory controlled by the Triballi, finally arriving at the River Lyginus, three days march from the Danube. Arrian then tells us that Syrmus, king of the Triballi, had known of Alexander's movements for some time and had evacuated a part of his army to Peuce Island. The rest of the Triballian army circled behind Alexander, taking up a position on the River Lyginus.[175] Syrmus shows an impressive appreciation of the need for military intelligence in an age when it was often very limited, as well as strategic thinking by moving his troops into position to outflank Alexander several days before the expected battle. Once Alexander had learned that the Triballi had taken up a position on his lines of supply and communication, he simply turned the army around and marched back to the River Lyginus to engage the enemy. The Macedonians took this in their stride, showing no signs of distress or panic. This obviously has a parallel with the Issus campaign where exactly the same was to happen. Again, the discipline of the Macedonian troops, as well as the allied contingents, is impressive. This simple but decisive action caught the Triballi unprepared; they reacted by fleeing to the protection of a wooded glen close to the river. Alexander deployed his heavy infantry in column; this is a most curious formation to adopt, but the intention was to avoid striking fear into the lightly-armed Triballi. If the heavy infantry were arrayed in the usual order of battle, it is unlikely that the Triballi would have met them in open combat. This would have meant that the problems in this region would have been suppressed, but not quelled.

Arrayed in front of the heavy infantry were the archers and slingers, with orders to advance 'at the double and discharge their missiles in the hope of drawing the enemy from the shelter of the wood into open ground'.[176] This is the first instance of a strategy that Alexander was to re-apply at every opportunity: to draw the enemy onto ground of Alexander's choosing.[177] Once the enemy had been drawn out of the woods, Philotas attacked the right wing with the cavalry from upper Macedonia, and Heraclides and Sopolis deployed to attack the left with the cavalry from Bottiaea and Amphipolis. Arrian tells us that the Triballi were holding their own until the heavy infantry joined the battle; after that the enemy were quickly routed, with 3,000 being killed.

After the battle Alexander marched north, reaching the Danube in three days and arriving at a prearranged rendezvous with part of the fleet. The fleet must have been dispatched from Macedonia at the outset of the campaign and this probably explains why Alexander's pace was so leisurely: he wanted to give the fleet time to arrive. This is an excellent example of Alexander's forward planning and realization that supply was a major factor in any successful campaign.

Getae

On the north bank of the Danube a large force of Getae had gathered: 4,000 cavalry and 10,000 infantry according to Arrian. Alexander ordered tents to be filled with hay and all available water-borne transport to be used to ferry troops over the river during the night. Hay-filled tents being used as makeshift rafts occur again at the crossing of the Oxus in 329.[178] Alexander was also probably aware of a precedent for the use of this kind of transportation in Xenophon.[179] Night-time river crossings were to become relatively commonplace during Alexander's career. Using this method Alexander ferried 1,500 cavalry and 4,000 infantry across the river that night. Alexander began by having his heavy infantry use their spears to flatten the grain, thus partially creating the battlefield upon which he wanted to fight. Note the use of 'spears' and not 'sarissas': another possible example of Alexander's heavy infantry being equipped as standard hoplites. It was probably easier to carry a spear on a makeshift raft than it would have been a sarissa. Once on the open plain the infantry took up their usual central location with Alexander and the cavalry on the right. The Getae broke quickly after a rapid cavalry charge timed to coincide with an infantry advance on an extended front. Arrian tells us the Getae were badly shaken by Alexander's crossing of the Danube with such a large force during the night, by his rapid attack and by the 'fearful sight of the phalanx advancing upon them in a solid mass'.[180]

It is precisely this fearful reaction that Alexander had wanted to avoid in the earlier battle against the Triballi; there he advanced in a narrow column, here on a wide front, and the difference of effect is evident. The Getae fled to their city, four miles away, but this was quickly sacked. Upon the return to the Danube, Alexander received the surrender of Syrmus and the Triballi on Peuce Island.

The timing of the campaign against the Getae is of interest. We know Alexander set off from Amphipolis in early April, that the crossing of the Danube and the campaign against the Getae did not occur until around June, and that Thebes was not sacked until October. Thus this part of the campaign took around two months and the entire Balkan campaign took four months; unlike many of his later operations, Alexander seemed to be in no hurry at all.

Upon re-crossing the Danube, Alexander received information that Cleitus, son of Bardylus, was in revolt and had been joined by Glaucias of the Taulantians, and further that the Autariates were planning to attack Alexander whilst he was on the march. Alexander, seeking allies, set off for his long time friend Langaros of the Agrianes. In terms of general geography, the Paeones were north of Macedonia between the Vardar and Strymon Rivers, with the Agrianes occupying the north-eastern area of Paeonia. Cleitus probably ruled the Dardani, who lived between the Drin and Erigon on Macedonia's northern border, the modern area of Kosovo, and the Autariatae were located to the north of Albania.

Pellium

Upon arriving at Pellium, possibly the capital of the Dardani, Alexander made camp by the River Eordiacus with the intention of assaulting the city on the following morning. Cleitus had taken up a position both inside the city and on the heights that ringed it to the northeast and southeast. This did not quite give him the ability to surround the Macedonians on every side as Arrian suggests. The following morning Alexander advanced towards the town and forced those troops in the hills to withdraw to the city after an extremely brief encounter. Alexander then chose to blockade the city by means of a circumvallation.[181] This strongly indicated either that the city was inaccessible for traditional siege equipment, or that he did not have his full siege train with him. The following day Glaucias arrived with the Taulantians, apparently in force, leaving Alexander in a very exposed position. He could not press the attack on the city for fear the Taulanteans would attack his flanks, and he could not attack this new, much larger force for fear of a sortie from the city. If Alexander knew of the imminent arrival of Glaucias, then to advance upon the city was a significant tactical mistake; if he did not, this is an example of the generally poor quality of intelligence in ancient warfare.

Alexander could not easily withdraw without significant risk, so he decided upon a display of force reminiscent of the Red Army in Moscow. The heavy infantry were initially drawn up with a 'depth of 120 files', which would give a frontage of 100 men.[182] There are two movements described in Arrian: the first involved the change from a box to a spearhead formation as they approached the Taulantians to the north. That this manoeuvre was conducted in absolute silence is a testimony to the discipline of the Macedonian heavy infantry. This march encouraged the Dardanians in the southern hills to attack Alexander's flanks. The heavy infantry, *en masse*, then turned 180 degrees and evidently reformed their square. Upon achieving this they raised a battle cry that was enough to route the Dardanians without a blow being struck.[183]

Seizing their opportunity the Macedonians then retreated towards the pass and the River Eordiacus beyond, with the hypaspists and Companion Cavalry leading the way. Upon seeing Alexander's main forces crossing the river, the Taulantians attempted an attack, but the retreat was covered by archers in mid-stream and arrow-throwing ballistae. The Macedonians then marched a few miles from the pass, feigning further retreat, after which they made camp and waited for three days. After this delay, Alexander returned to the River Eordiacus, crossed it during the night with the Agrianians, archers and the *taxeis* of Perdiccas and Coenus and engaged the Illyrians whilst they were apparently still in their beds; the city of Pellium fell soon afterwards. We should juxtapose this slaughter with Alexander's response to Parmenio at Gaugamela. When Parmenio suggested a similar night attack, Alexander responded: 'I will not demean myself by stealing victory like a thief. Alexander must defeat his enemies openly and honestly'.[184]

Balkan Campaign: Observations

Alexander's Balkan campaign provides us with the first opportunity to examine Alexander's generalship without the safety net of Philip, or even of Parmenio, who was with the advance force in Asia Minor. The campaign is worthy of praise, but was not without significant mistakes. The assertion that there is no trace of development in Alexander's generalship is certainly not the case. During this campaign, Alexander showed none of the speed and lightning marches that characterized his later campaigns. His greatest mistake, however, was in allowing himself to become trapped in the plain outside of Pellium; we can only speculate that in later years he would have left a column to besiege Pellium whilst he set off to defeat the Taulantians on ground of his own choosing, rather than allowing them to link up. If the intention of this campaign was to pacify Macedonia's northern borders, then it can be considered a spectacular success.

The Campaign of Issus

The region of Cilicia is encircled on three sides by mountain ranges, and on the fourth side is the sea, making access to the central plain difficult if opposed. To the north and west is the Taurus range; to the east of the central plain lies the Amanus range which forms an almost impenetrable barrier, given the scarcity of passes.

Alexander began the campaign by a lightning march towards and through the 'Cilician Gates' and so entered Cilicia, probably around the end of May, assuming no earlier delay at Gordium or Ancyra. The region was to become his base of operations for the next several months. After forcing the pass, Alexander arrived at Tarsus before Arsames, the Persian commander of the region. Apparently Alexander had feared that Arsames would institute a scorched earth policy such as had been advocated by Memnon before the Granicus. After failing to secure Tarsus, however, Arsames appears to have withdrawn from the region without any major damage: the scorched earth policy was again not used. Apparently the Persian defenders were in the process of burning the city as Alexander's light-armed troops arrived, the fires being quickly extinguished.

Whilst at Tarsus Alexander fell seriously ill, the result of a swim in the freezing waters of the Cnydus River. The illness apparently incapacitated him for several weeks, although he eventually made a full recovery after the ministrations of Philip the Acarnanian, his doctor. Whilst Alexander was recovering, he sent Parmenio south to secure a number of key passes out of Cilicia. The army had most likely been divided as it passed through the Cilician Gates, Alexander taking a small contingent to Tarsus, whilst Parmenio took most of the rest south. Parmenio seems to have spent perhaps as much as a month in southern Cilicia, before returning to Alexander at Castabalum.[185]

Once Alexander had recovered, he marched southwest to Anchialus and Soli, where he levied a fine of 200 silver talents upon the inhabitants for their loyalty to Persia. In order to quell unrest in the hills around Soli, Alexander took three *taxeis* of heavy infantry, the Agrianians and archers and conducted a seven day campaign against hill tribesmen in the so called 'Rough Cilicia' region: Alexander was evidently not yet worried about Darius, as we hear of no efforts to locate him. At the completion of the 'Rough Cilicia' campaign, Alexander further divided the army into two columns: the first commanded by Philotas, the second by himself.[186] Alexander's column advanced upon Magarsus and nearby Mallus, which submitted without incident. Interestingly, unlike Soli, Mallus was not fined, no doubt because it was in a strategically far more sensitive area. It was whilst Alexander was encamped at Mallus that he received news that Darius was only two days march away at Sochi.

We know, then, that Parmenio was sent south before Alexander occupied Tarsus in order to capture the Issus plain and the passes leading out of Cilicia to the south - specifically the Pillar of Jonah and the Beilan Pass. We must now establish the timeline for Darius' arrival at Sochi and his occupation of the aforementioned southern passes. This is no easy task given that none of our sources actually synchronize Alexander's movements with those of Darius. We know from Curtius that the Persian contingents from the furthest parts of the empire were not summoned because of Darius' great haste.[187] We do not possess much data on the timeframe of this period, but if Darius marched out immediately upon hearing of the death of Memnon, he would have arrived at Sochi around the end of September.

The timeline is just as confusing for the Macedonian side as for the Persians, but it seems certain that there are around four months unaccounted for, during which we simply have no certainty of where Alexander was or what he was doing. There are two possible solutions: either Alexander's illness was far more serious than we know; or Alexander paused at Gordium for longer than we had previously believed, no doubt being worried about the progress of Persian operations in the Aegean. The reality is probably some combination of the two.

The strategic decisions of both sides were greatly affected, not only by the passes to the south of Issus, but by those to the northeast as well. When Darius took the decision to move north and circle in behind Alexander, he had to cross the Amanus Mountains somewhere. The modern road and rail networks in the region probably run along the same lines as the ancient passes. With this in mind, there are only two passes large enough to take an army through in relatively short time and in good order; these are the Hasanbeyli Pass and the Bahce Pass. The Hasanbeyli Pass, the more southerly of the two, carries the modern road over the mountains, whilst the Bahce Pass carries the Baghdad railway. Both of these passes are around 1,200m. We do not know which pass Darius used, it could equally easily have been either one.

When Darius arrived at Sochi, he was in an ideal position to take advantage of his superior numbers. He was in a wide open plain that could not be more suited to his superiority in cavalry; although that, in itself, would not have guaranteed victory, given that this is what occurred at Gaugamela and Darius was still defeated. Why would Darius abandon such an ideal position in favour of the confines of the Issus plain? The sources are unanimous in blaming Darius' impatience.[188] The delay was because of Alexander's illness, but Darius was convinced by the argument that Alexander was a coward and would not come to meet him. Curtius has a debate on the subject of dividing the army to trap Alexander in a pincer, although this is a theme that does not appear in either Arrian or Plutarch.

It is also no doubt true that Darius' supplies were running low; the plain around Sochi could only support his massive host for a short time.[189]

Final Stages of the Prelude to Battle

We can presume that Alexander was reasonably well informed of Darius' movements from Parmenio who was occupying the southern passes, but what of Darius' intelligence? The inhabitants of the region of Cilicia were not Greek and had no particular reason to welcome Alexander. Both Diodorus and Curtius tell us that the locals were generally not supportive of the Macedonian presence.[190] Persian supporters in Soli could easily have travelled by boat up the Orontes River to report Alexander's location and activities to Darius. There seems little doubt that coastal towns had significant fishing fleets; we know that Alexander had no difficulty in finding a ship at Myriandrus to verify Darius' position behind him.

Darius would have known that Alexander was conducting a campaign with part of his force in 'Rough Cilicia'. He would also have learned from the guards he had posted at the southern passes that Parmenio had moved into this area. From the guards he more than likely posted at the northern passes, he would have received no information about the Macedonians at all. This data would have quite reasonably led Darius to conclude that Alexander's forces were divided roughly in two, and that he had an opportunity to drive a wedge between them – but only if he acted quickly. Darius' strategy would only have a chance if he was able to march considerably faster than he had in the approach to Sochi; he therefore dispatched his baggage train south to Damascus. We also know of a night march by Darius, the march in which the two armies passed each other during the hours of darkness. The story of the two armies passing each other is very dubious, but the idea of the Persians making a night march need not be automatically rejected.

This passage of Plutarch is crucial: 'during the night they missed one another and both turned back'.[191] We frequently read in modern sources of the brilliance of Alexander in simply turning his army around to face the threat from Darius, but it would seem that Darius himself did exactly the same. Plutarch goes on to say: 'Darius was no less eager to extricate his forces from the mountain passes and regain his former camping ground in the plain'.[192]

This would seem to support the theory that Darius intended to drive a wedge between the two elements of Alexander's army; realizing that he had been too slow, however, he wished to recover his former position at Sochi but was unable to do so as Alexander brought him to battle rapidly from this point. Darius' innovative strategy had failed, perhaps only by a few hours.

Darius took out his frustration upon the Macedonian field hospital at Issus, mutilating those whom Alexander had left behind. Darius now realized that he could not extricate himself from the area safely and so turned south to meet Alexander on the Plain of Issus, on the banks of the Pinarus River. Despite the failure of his strategy, Darius was still in a strong position, sitting, as he was, across Alexander's lines of supply and communication. With this in mind, Darius moved south from Issus on the day following the massacre and made preparations on the banks of the Pinarus River.[193]

Upon hearing that Darius was at Issus, Alexander evidently did not initially believe his scouts and so dispatched a part of the Companions on a ship from Myriandrus to verify the report. Once verified, he simply turned his army around and made for the river. This is, as frequently noted, a fine example of the discipline of the Macedonian army.[194]

Before going on to discuss the battle itself, there is one final element of the preliminary movements that we must understand: why did Alexander move south of the pillar of Jonah? Why did he not remain on the Plain of Issus to await Darius? As at the Granicus, we have two entirely different accounts of Alexander's strategy. Arrian presents the campaign as purely and entirely offensive. Curtius, on the other hand, has Alexander adopting a defensive posture, essentially on the advice of Parmenio, just prior to the battle. On this reading, we have two mutually incompatible accounts, but this is only true if the account of Arrian is accepted and I believe that it is essentially a misinterpretation of the text. Arrian presents Alexander as moving to Myriandrus, from which point he would move to engage Darius at Sochi. Curtius likewise has Alexander move south of the Pillar of Jonah, out of the Plain of Issus and into the much smaller area of the Plain of Myriandrus. This is an area enclosed by mountains and passes on all sides: specifically, the Pillar of Jonah to the north and the Beilan Pass to the east. Arrian tells us:[195]

He [Alexander] at once called a meeting of his staff and told them this important news [that Darius was still at Sochi]. They urged unanimously an immediate advance. Alexander thanked them and dismissed the meeting, and on the following day moved forward with the evident intention of Attack. Two days later he took up a position at Myriandrus, and during the night there was a storm of such violent wind and rain that he was compelled to remain where he was, with no chance of breaking camp.

Alexander could not have been intending to advance to Sochi to engage Darius, as he moved southwest once through the Pillar of Jonah, towards Myriandrus, not southeast towards the Beilan pass and ultimately to Sochi. The storm that caused the delay is also puzzling. There is no hint of a storm in any of the other sources, and no hint in Arrian that the storm delayed the progress of the Persians who had to cover in excess of 130 km from Sochi to Issus via the northern passes in a very short period of time. The storm could easily be an apologetic fiction used by Arrian to delay Alexander and allow Darius to appear behind him, essentially covering up the fact that Alexander was conducting a defensive campaign as presented in Curtius. Alexander in fact had no intention of being drawn into a battle on Darius' terms. As in almost all of his campaigns, the battle was to be fought on ground of Alexander's choosing. Alexander, therefore, moved towards Myriandrus because it was far more defensible than the Issus plain: it was far smaller and Myriandrus was closer to the key passes to the east and west than Issus was to the passes to the north and south. A camp at Myriandrus, therefore, could easily defend the plain.

Whilst a certain identification of the river with the Pinarus is not possible, the Kuru Cay, 3km north of the Payas, is the most reasonable assumption for the site of the battle. With regards to the battlefield itself, we know from Callisthenes that the Plain of Issus was fourteen stades from the coast to the foothills of the Amanus Mountains, and we know that the river flowed at right angles to both.[196] Callisthenes also tells us that the river was difficult to cross, possessing precipitous banks along the whole of its length: the river and its banks presented Darius with a strong defensive position from which to await Alexander.

The Battle of Issus

Once Darius had advanced to the Plain of Issus, taking up a position at the Pinarus River, Arrian presents us with a picture of Alexander being shocked and not believing in his scouting reports. When the reality of these reports had been established, Alexander made a speech to his troops, as he frequently did, to fire the blood of his troops before advancing.[197]

Alexander's final advance towards the Persians was in three stages. The first involved the recapture of the coastal defiles with units of light cavalry and archers. This was the route that the Macedonians would have to traverse in order to reach the Issus plain. The reminder of the army was instructed to rest and eat their final meal before the coming battle. The second stage of the advance occurred after nightfall when Alexander and the remaining elements of the army moved to occupy the Pillar of Jonah. The passage was secured around midnight, and the men were allowed to rest for the remainder of the night. The third and final stage began at the third trumpet call, just before dawn the following morning, when the whole army marched in column along the coast road. As the army advanced out of the foothills, and as space began to open up, the frontage was gradually extended as heavy infantry were brought up, one *taxis* at a time, until the Greek right was touching the foothills to the east and the left of the line was touching the sea coast. The use of the heavy infantry to the front of the column, and the lack of mention of lighter troops, is unusual and an indication that Alexander may have expected to be attacked while on the march. He was evidently far from certain that Darius would actually wait for him at the Pinarus, and so had to be prepared for that eventuality. As the heavy infantry entered the plain, the infantry were able to deploy in battle array, at first thirty-two ranks deep, thinning to sixteen and finally eight ranks.[198]

Alexander's primary tactical problem was how to effect a penetration of the Persian line without himself being outflanked, a problem that recurs in every one of Alexander's set-piece battles, particularly given that he was always greatly outnumbered.[199] At Issus the sea provided a natural barrier and thus protection to his left flank, with the mountains doing much the same on his right. Initially Parmenio was woefully ill equipped on the left to perform a defensive action against the massed Persian cavalry, only commanding the Allied Greek cavalry. The heavy infantry was, as always, deployed in the centre according to a strictly adhered-to code of honour. To the right of this, again in accordance with the standard deployment, were the hypaspists under Nicanor, son of Parmenio. Initially the Thessalian cavalry, the Companion Cavalry, the Paeonians and the *prodromoi* were all deployed on the right wing. This constituted the bulk of the cavalry at Alexander's disposal, and certainly all of the quality mounted troops in the Macedonian order of battle. Alexander's tactics were startlingly simple: to launch a massive cavalry strike at the Persian left and break through before his own left wing folded. The initial set up made this strategy a massive gamble that Alexander evidently realized and quickly rectified by sending the Thessalians over to the left with Parmenio. The movement occurred behind the front line and so was shielded from the Persians, who may not have realized that the left had been strengthened at the onset of battle; initially there had been 4,500 cavalry on the right and only 600 on the left.

By the time Alexander arrived on the battlefield, Darius had already deployed his troops and was waiting. Darius had evidently studied Alexander's dispositions at the Granicus and expected Alexander to deploy in the same way. To counter the central strength of the Macedonian heavy infantry he deployed his only quality infantry in the centre, the now-depleted Greek mercenary troops, under the command of Thymondas. The Greek mercenaries were stationed along a stretch of banks between 500m and 1.6km from the coast. The banks were steep in this sector and an attack from cavalry was highly unlikely. Deploying Greek mercenary troops in this area was tactically very sound indeed; the steep banks would make an assault by cavalry impossible and would severely disrupt the Macedonian heavy infantry. In order to bolster the defensive strength, he created several abatis, essentially temporary defensive palisades, at the most vulnerable points. Arrian and Curtius, following Callisthenes, both give the strength of the Greek mercenary force at 30,000; this simply cannot be possible given the losses in battle, captives from the Granicus and the inevitable desertions that would have occurred.[200] They were stationed opposite the hypaspists and *pezhetairoi*, who themselves numbered 12,000. As the Greeks did not seriously overlap the Macedonians we can assume that, if their depth was the same as their opponents, their numbers would also have been similar. However, that can not be taken as an argument for assuming similar numbers. It is well known that hoplites could have a depth of fifty or more on occasion, so if the lines were of similar lengths and yet the Persians had much greater numbers, then their files would be deeper. We simply can not know the size of the Persian force, but can only assume it was at least as great as Alexander's.

Arrian shows little interest in the Persians, with the exception the Greek mercenary infantry and of the Cardaces, whom he describes as hoplites, clearly believing them to be heavy infantry. Arrian states clearly that the Cardaces were stationed to either side of the Greek mercenaries and numbered 60,000.[201] Given the limitations of space in the plain, and the large mass of cavalry by the sea, it seems highly unlikely that Arrian could be correct that the Cardaces were posted to either side of the Greek mercenaries. The Cardaces are highly likely to be associated with the peltasts of Callisthenes. These peltasts were stationed along the mid-section of the Pinarus River, between 1.6km and 3.5km from the coast.

If we are right in associating the Cardaces with the peltasts, then they were certainly not hoplites; nor are they an attempt by the Persians to develop a native force that could oppose Greek hoplites. Having said this we must remember that the Macedonian *pezhetairoi* and hypaspists were essentially peltasts themselves, possessing very little defensive armour and only a small shield (*pelte*). Given that they are almost always referred to as a phalanx, and therefore often assumed to be heavy infantry, we should not be too quick to label the Cardaces. Expressions like 'heavy infantry', 'light infantry', 'peltasts' and 'skirmishers' assume conclusions about their abilities and likely deployment which are not always valid.

The Persians, then, deployed their heavy cavalry on the extreme right, commanded by Nabarzanes, screened by a group of slingers and archers. Next to these were the Greek mercenary infantry in their prepared defensive position as mentioned above. Next to these were the Cardaces of an unknown number, perhaps 20,000 strong or slightly more given the size of their frontage, commanded by Aristomedes, a Thessalian mercenary. Next to these were detachments of Hyrcanian and Median cavalry along with a group of unspecified Persian cavalry and a detachment of javelinmen and slingers deployed in front of them. The Persians also employed a reserve line behind the front, 40,000 strong according to Curtius.[202] Arrian is cautious about giving the total number of Persian troops as 600,000, reporting it as hearsay, although Plutarch gives the same figure.[203] Diodorus and Justin report 400,000 infantry and 100,000 cavalry, whilst Curtius gives the lowest estimate: 250,000 infantry and 62,000 cavalry.[204] All of these estimates may be too high but it is likely that Alexander was, as usual, heavily outnumbered.

Curtius explicitly lays out Darius' tactics for the battle: he at first intended to occupy the foothills with a force in excess of 20,000, intending to make an encircling movement 'both in the front and in the rear'.[205] On the seaward flank he apparently planned a similar operation. Darius, therefore, planned a double encirclement that would press Alexander from every direction. The strategy was sound if the topography allowed for it, as it had for the Persians at Cunaxa, or would do at Gaugamela. At Issus, however, the plain was narrow and Alexander's flanks were protected by the sea to the west and the Amanus Mountains to the east; Alexander had lured Darius to the Issus plain for this very reason.

Darius was no fool and realized that the plain was unsuitable for the double envelopment that he had planned and he modified his tactics accordingly. There were several changes to the preferred double envelopment plan; firstly the strong defensive position along the river bank, already discussed. The second change was far more complex and involved two phases. In the first, the advance guard of the Persian army, consisting of cavalry 20,000 strong, archers and some light infantry, were to harass the Macedonian column on the seaward side as it advanced onto the plain.[206] This sound stratagem was disrupted by Alexander deploying his heavy infantry in deep order to cover his deployment. The second phase was to feign the envelopment strategy that was his original intention; this should have had the effect of pinning Alexander's flank to his centre in case the attack materialized. Alexander was in no mood to play Darius' games, however; he quickly launched a cavalry attack against this weak force and routed it, thus eliminating the threat entirely.

Darius tried to open the battle by sending a unit of cavalry across the ford on his left wing. It very quickly became apparent that this strategy was flawed; the narrowness of the ford and steepness of the banks made the attack difficult. Arrian tells us that these troops were quickly withdrawn without an engagement and the bulk of the Persian cavalry strength was transferred to the Persian right, where their weight of numbers would be more of a factor, along with the more positive terrain.[207]

As a reaction to the Persian changes in disposition, Alexander moved the Thessalian cavalry to his left to defend the coastline. It is possible that Alexander had always intended to deploy the Thessalians on the left, as he did in every major engagement, and the fact that the transfer had not occurred before this point is simply an indication of the physical lack of space in that sector. The deployment would have to have waited until the infantry was sufficiently far enough advanced to allow for the deployment.

The movement of the Thessalians caused Alexander to re-examine the tactical situation on his right flank. In that sector he now posted the *prodromoi*, Paeonian cavalry and the Macedonian archers, next to the

Companion Cavalry. Beyond these were deployed the highly-specialized Agrianians and an unknown unit of cavalry. This final group on the right wing was drawn up at an angle to the front line and were a prototype of the flank guards that were so crucial to Alexander's success at the Battle of Gaugamela. Alexander seems to have expected the right wing to lose its cohesion as it chased down those Persians in the foothills. This is evidently something that he was not overly concerned with; Alexander frequently and deliberately allowed the army to lose its cohesion by separating off sections, but only if it served his tactical purpose, as it did at the Granicus and the Hydaspes for example.

The tactical situation on the left was far less complex; The Thracian javelinmen under Sitalces, and the Cretan archers, were stationed to the left of the heavy infantry, forming a flank guard of their own as well as a link with the Greek allied cavalry.[208] This force was entirely inadequate to the task of resisting the charge of the massed Persian cataphracts that opposed them and hence their reinforcement by the Thessalians. (Curtius and Arrian both tell us that both horse and rider in the Persian heavy cavalry were covered with plate armour, hence my slightly anachronistic use of the term 'cataphract': it is generic enough for our purposes here.[209]) The finest of the Persian heavy cavalry were the Saca horsemen who played a significant role at Gaugamela. The Bactrian and Sogdianian cavalry were not present at Issus, and the heavy cavalry mentioned there were probably Parthian. There were definitely Hyrcanian cavalry present at Issus and it is reasonable to assume the Parthians would also be present given that they seem to have formed a single satrapy.[210]

From the Persian perspective, Darius' plan to outflank Alexander by deploying troops in the foothills was entirely sensible, but failed completely due to Alexander's frequently-demonstrated ability to react to the fluid situation presented by a battlefield. Having said this, the tactical situation on the opposite wing was developing well for Darius. The sources differ widely on the detail of the engagement in this sector: Arrian considers the engagement to have been of very little significance, a mere adjunct to the fighting in the centre and on Alexander's right. Arrian states that:[211]

> The Persian cavalry facing Alexander's Thessalian's refused, once the battle had developed, to remain inactive on the further side of the stream, but charged across in a furious onslaught on the Thessalian squadrons.

The fighting was undoubtedly fierce and the Persians did not give way until they saw Darius flee in the centre. Once this was achieved then there was a general rout on the part of the Persians. It was in this phase of the battle that the Persians suffered their most serious losses. Arrian's reduction of the significance of the role of the Thessalians and Parmenio in the battle is the result of a long series of attempts by Ptolemy, his favoured source, to reduce the significance of Parmenio whilst glorifying Alexander's role in the battle.

Curtius' account is somewhat different; in this version the battle actually began on the Macedonian left wing.[212] Curtius tells us explicitly that the Persians attacked along the shoreline against the Peloponnesian and Greek allied cavalry before the Thessalians arrived; on this interpretation their move would be a reaction to this opening Persian gambit. Curtius also tells us that the Peloponnesians and allied Greeks may have inadvertently begun the battle by straying into range of the Persians.[213]

> They had now come within javelin range when the Persian cavalry made a furious charge on the left wing of their enemy.

Curtius goes on to tell us that:[214]

> When the Macedonian saw this he ordered two *ilai* to maintain a position on the ridge while he promptly transferred the rest to the heart of the danger. Then he withdrew the Thessalian cavalry from the fighting line, telling their commander to pass unobtrusively behind the Macedonian rear and join Parmenio.

It seems probable that Curtius used a source biased towards Parmenio, whilst that of Arrian demonstrated an anti-Parmenio stance.

Alexander seems to have been using his weak Peloponnesian and Allied Greek cavalry as bait to draw the Persians into battle. This tactic of using a relatively weak body of cavalry as bait to draw a stronger force of enemy cavalry onto unfavourable ground and into a position where they could be exposed to a flanking attack by other, stronger Macedonian units is a regular feature of Alexander's battles. At the Granicus in the previous year, Alexander essentially sacrificed an advanced unit of cavalry in order to throw the Persian cavalry guarding the ford into confusion and disarray. At Gaugamela, two years after Issus, Alexander ordered the mercenary cavalry to attack the vastly superior Bactrian and Scythian cavalry. In this instance the stratagem was relatively simple, but it was a tried and tested one. The allied Greek cavalry did not have to 'sell a fake', perhaps making only a slight feint; the Persian cataphracts were evidently eager to attack a seemingly-weak enemy. The result of this Persian overconfidence was that they exposed their flanks to 1,800 elite Thessalian heavy cavalry, thus falling neatly into Alexander's cleverly-laid trap.

This tactic of Alexander's was simple yet devastatingly effective and it was one which Alexander perfected and modified to the specific terrain and tactical situation of each battle. It is this kind of adaptability, the ability to fight in all conditions and all terrains, that marks Alexander out as a military genius.

In contrast to the complexity on the left, the battle on the right was far less innovative. Arrian gives us a view of a spectacular cavalry charge, using the simile of the line surging forward like a wave to fall upon the enemy.[215] This view may contain an amount of literary merit, but is historically entirely incorrect. Topographically there was simply no room for the battle that Arrian describes. It seems far more likely that the Persian left was driven back from the ford by a combination of the cavalry and light infantry units on Alexander's right.

Once the Persian troops in the foothills were routed, the cavalry in that sector charged across the river. The *prodromoi* and Paeonians probably attacked first because they were a little less encumbered by armour and thus more mobile. They would have been supported by light infantry such as the Agrianians in their initial assault, again as at the Granicus.

Once the light cavalry, supported by the Agrianians and archers, had forced the crossing, they held the enemy at bay while the Companions forded the river, *ile* by *ile* and then formed up in their familiar wedge formations. Once they were formed up, they took over from the light cavalry and charged the remaining enemy in that area in the face of defensive fire from the nearby Persian archers. Darius had weakened his left in order to deliver what he hoped would be a hammer blow against the supposedly-weak Macedonian left flank; this decision proved fatal. The Persian left quickly melted away under the onslaught of the fresh Companion Cavalry. As so often, once the Companions broke through the Persian lines they wheeled towards the centre and made a flanking attack. This manoeuvre was a hallmark of Alexander, and in this instance it was perfectly timed to coincide with the attack of the heavy infantry in the centre. The shock of the Macedonian heavy infantry attack across the river, combined with a flanking attack by Alexander and the Companion Cavalry, was simply too much for the Persian centre to handle. They quickly began to retreat, and retreat became a rout, with the slaughter that ensued.[216]

Darius' strategy was sound. He evidently planned for a strong defence in the centre, aided by the abatis that he set up along the less steep banks of the river. It is clear that his tactics were not purely defensive, however, given his positioning of troops in the foothills with the intention of outflanking Alexander's right. His final plan to attack Alexander in strength along the coast shows Darius adapting to what he saw as the evolving tactical situation of the battlefield; he believed that an opportunity had presented itself to deliver a decisive blow down that wing. The fact that this move failed utterly was more to do with Alexander's supreme planning, foresight and adaptability, than any tactical or strategic deficiency on the part of Darius.

When assessing Alexander, we can see in the Battle of Issus his supreme strategic and tactical ability. Firstly in drawing the Persians onto terrain that was best suited to his army, as he so often did, and secondly in the execution of the battle itself. In this battle we see a series of quite brilliant flanking manouevres, starting with the cavalry on the left luring the Persians forward to be outflanked by the Thessalians moving in from the right to execute a brilliantly-planned trap. We also see Alexander forcing a crossing on the extreme right of the formation, then wheeling left to flank the Persian guard defending Darius. Finally we see the hypaspists and the two right-hand *pezhetairoi taxeis* moving to their right to force a crossing of the river, then the *pezhetairoi* swinging left to flank the Greek mercenary infantry at the same time as they were being attacked from the front by the rest of the heavy infantry. Finally we have the hypaspists, once across the river, swinging to the right to attack Darius in the opposing flank to Alexander and the Companion Cavalry.

Tyre

The escape of Darius after the devastating defeat at Issus presented Alexander with a major strategic decision: should he pursue Darius into the Persian heartlands or continue his policy of defeating the Persian navy on land by heading south towards Egypt? To pursue Darius would be to leave the major Persian strongholds of Phoenicia and Egypt unconquered, as well as leaving the still active Persian fleet with bases from which to potentially take the battle to Greece, as had been Memnon's strategy the previous year. From the modern perspective, the decision looks difficult, but for Alexander it was not. He immediately set off south along the Phoenician coast towards Tyre and ultimately Egypt. He evidently felt that Darius was of no immediate danger and that having defeated him once he could do so again. Alexander also may have felt it wise to prevent any possibility of a Persian invasion of Greece whilst also securing the grain supply from Egypt.

Once news of Issus spread, the Phoenician cities in Alexander's path, such as Byblos and Sidon, surrendered largely without a struggle. It initially appeared that Tyre would also follow suit: as Alexander approached the city he was met by a delegation of representatives offering peaceful terms with the Macedonian conqueror. The Tyrians, safe in their island stronghold, were willing to accept alliance with Alexander, but not subjugation.[217] To Alexander the two were virtually one and the same: he thanked them for their offer and instructed them to make preparations for him to make sacrifice in the Temple of Heracles within the city.[218] The Tyrians wished to remain neutral and refused Alexander's request, but stated that they would also refuse any Persian access to the city. In this way they felt that they would be safe from both the Macedonians and the Persians. As part of the peace deal they also offered Alexander the opportunity to sacrifice in another temple in Old Tyre, on the mainland.[219] Alexander's reaction to such a snub was entirely predictable: he flew into a violent rage that is reported by both Arrian and Curtius; the latter likened it to an irrational temper tantrum, stating that 'Alexander lost his temper, which he also failed to control on other occasions'.[220]

Alexander may have anticipated the Tyrian response and used it as a pretext for storming the city, but he seldom shows any indication of needing a pretext before conducting military operations. The Tyrian motivation to attempt to resist the man who had so recently defeated the Great King is initially difficult to fathom, but Curtius stresses the Tyrians' utter belief in the impregnability of their island fortress, especially given Alexander's lack of any significant navy. Diodorus takes a rather different line, however; he saw the Tyrian resistance as part of a coordinated Persian grand strategy of resistance to Alexander's seemingly-unstoppable march.[221] This seems unlikely largely because the Persian high command would have been in tatters after Issus and not in a position to develop a coherent strategy. The Tyrians seem sincere in simply not wishing to be subjects of Alexander.

The fortress of Tyre was superbly sited for defence; it lay on an island that was separated from the mainland by a 750m stretch of water. Although the straight was quite wide, it was relatively shallow to within a couple of hundred metres of the island; at that point the seabed fell away quite dramatically to around three fathoms in depth. The supreme confidence evidently felt by the Tyrians in their position was bolstered by a delegation from distant Carthage, a foundation of Tyre, who promised military aid.[222] Tyrian confidence was not founded simply on geography, but on their men and equipment too: catapults lined the walls, and *harpagones* were constructed to use against Alexander's siege engines along with 'ravens' and other defensive siege equipment. *Harpagones* were grappling irons, invented by Pericles according to Pliny. They were something new to Alexander, but certainly not new to Greek warfare. A *corvus* (Greek *korax*, meaning 'raven' or perhaps 'crow'), is not the complex grappling hook and boarding bridge made famous by Duilius in the first Punic War and described by Polyaenus; Curtius is imagining a simple grappling hook of the type used at Mycale in 479.[223]

Once the decision to besiege the island had been made, Alexander gathered his troops together in Old Tyre and issued one of his famous speeches.[224] Curtius tells us that its purpose was to overcome the reluctance of the troops to attack the island fortress, but the contents are not at all similar to those presented by Arrian. Whatever the contents, we can assume that it had the desired effect upon the men.

The defences of Tyre were legendary and it would no doubt have been known to Alexander that the city had withstood a siege lasting thirteen years by the Babylonian King Nebuchadnezzar in the sixth century. To a man like Alexander, however, this would have acted as a spur not a deterrent. Once the decision had been made to capture the city Alexander was faced with the very obvious question of how that was to be achieved. He possessed no significant navy at this point; the only option, therefore, was to construct a massive mole to connect the island to the mainland. The idea of a mole may have originated when Dionysius I used the same method in his siege of Motya in 397. One imagines Philip would either have agreed to the Tyrian terms, used some subterfuge to capture the city, or set about constructing a fleet: Alexander was not Philip.[225]

The initial stages of the construction of the mole occurred without any significant interference from Tyre; but the time and effort involved was prodigious. As the mole approached deeper water, closer to the fortress, the

Tyrians evidently started to become worried and were forced to start to take proactive actions against the Macedonians. Initially this came simply in the form of projectile weapons fired from the city, but quickly developed into naval action too. The construction teams then were coming under constant attack both from the walls and from seaborne raids at various points along the mole. In what can only be described as another remarkable feat of engineering, the Macedonians began building siege towers on the mole to help defend the construction teams. These towers were intended to be higher than the walls of the city in order to lay down a suppressing fire against the defenders on the walls from artillery pieces that had been placed in siege towers. Anticipating an incendiary attack, and learning from the mistake at Halicarnassus, the towers were covered with skins and hides to protect them.[226]

The construction teams working on the mole would not have been specialists drafted in for the job, but would mostly have been regular troops assigned to the role. This flexibility and adaptability of the troops is one of the fundamental reasons why Alexander was successful, although it is true to say this adaptability was more usually demonstrated on the battlefield. During the initial stages of the siege, the Tyrians showed themselves to be far more flexible and proactive in their defence than the Macedonians. The ingenuity of the Tyrians is clearly shown in their use of the device of the fire ship. They filled a transport vessel with brushwood and other flammable materials, and set up twin masts in its bows from each of which were suspended cauldrons of pitch. The vessel was heavily ballasted aft with rocks and sand, which meant the front of the vessel was out of the water, allowing it to run aground on the mole more easily. The fire ship was then towed towards the mole by means of triremes acting as tug boats.[227] As the fire ship drew close to the mole some specially selected crewmen set fire to the brushwood and dove overboard. The raging inferno that the ship quickly became soon spread and the siege towers caught fire and were completely destroyed.

After the incident Alexander gave orders to his engineers that the mole be widened and rebuilt. Arrian only twice makes reference to the famous siege engineers (here and at 2.21.1). None of our extant sources mention any of them by name, but we can probably assume that the Thessalian Diades, once famously described as 'the man who took Tyre with Alexander', was among them. Charias was probably also among them, the pupil of Polyeidus, Philip's engineer at the sieges of Perinthus and

Byzantium.[228] The extra space on the mole would be used to incorporate a greater number of siege towers. Palisades were also constructed along the banks of the mole to protect the construction teams from seaborne assault.

The Persian fleet was now effectively removed from the Persian order of battle, given that most of their home ports were in Alexander's hands. This was exactly the strategy that Alexander had espoused at Halicarnassus. The fleets of many former Persian cities now joined Alexander at Sidon: Gierostratus, king of Arabus and Enylus, king of Byblos, both arrived after leaving the fleet of Autophradates. On a single day, eighty Phoenician triremes arrived at Sidon, along with nine from Rhodes, three from Soli and Mallus, ten from Lycia and a fifty-oared vessel from Macedonia. Shortly after this the king of Cyprus arrived with 120 warships. Alexander willingly accepted all comers into his new expanding fleet, regardless of previous allegiances.[229]

During this part of the siege, as the Macedonians were busy reconstructing and expanding the mole, Alexander was evidently looking for a release of pent-up energy. Whilst the fleet was being organized, Alexander took some cavalry, the hypaspists, Agrianians and archers in an expedition into the Lebanese Mountains.[230] This detachment of troops is a familiar formula: these were the most versatile troops in the whole army and the ones capable of the most rapid movement across almost any terrain. The campaign was brief and we know little of it, but it did have the effect of sating Alexander's appetite for conquest for a short while.

Once Alexander had returned to Tyre, the siege was rejoined. The mole was almost at the walls of the city, but had not yet reached them. Alexander manned his new fleet with as many troops as was possible, either anticipating a naval battle that would be conducted along the same lines as a land battle or expecting that he would be able to assault the walls directly from the sea. This manning of his fleet again shows the flexibility of his army; those involved would almost certainly consist of the hypaspists and perhaps the Agrianians too.

Once the ships were manned, Alexander gave orders that the city be blockaded: the Cyprian contingent was stationed outside the northern harbour, the Phoenician navy to the south.[231] The mole had also reached the walls, allowing a direct attack against the city for the first time. Alexander was now in a position from which he could press on all sides; from this point, the history of Alexander's career tells us that it was only a matter of time for the defenders.

During the final stages of the assault we see some novel tactics from

Alexander. Curtius tells us that he was able to attack all sections of the outer walls simultaneously. This reference in Curtius, supported by Arrian, to all points around Tyre being attacked by artillery and rams is fundamental; it demonstrates that Alexander had equipped some of his triremes with stone-throwing catapults as well as rams, an ingenious strategy. Diodorus tells us that the catapults were used directly against the walls.[232] This is an important innovation as almost always before this point catapults would have been used to provide suppressive fire against the defenders, keeping them off the walls and allowing the infantry to scale ladders or use rams unhindered.[233] It has been argued that this was the first time in history that stone-throwing catapults were used in such a way, although this is almost certainly incorrect as they were used at Halicarnassus and, perhaps, even at Miletus shortly before that.[234]

Another innovative stratagem of Alexander was to construct siege towers on the decks of triremes; this allowed the battering rams to attack higher up the walls, where they would be thinner and thus weaker. The use of both catapults (for direct assault against the walls, combined with the suppressive fire they provided) and rams was an early combined-arms force. The catapults provided covering fire for the rams and marines as the walls were stormed. The troop transport ships were equipped with a novel type of scaling ladder.[235] The ladders that Alexander's engineers created seem to have been raised by means of a specially-constructed wooden turret. Alexander was using the kind of land-based tactics that had proved so successful, the integrated use of a variety of troop types, and adapting it to a new environment; something that he did time and again during his career. The strategy would not have been successful, however, without a well-trained and flexible army coupled with extremely talented engineers.

The defenders were equally ingenious: they erected wooden towers to rain missiles down upon the attackers, seemingly at all points around the circuit of the city; fire arrows were used against the Phoenician ships and their crews became too afraid to approach within range. Diodorus describes windmills that were used to deflect projectiles thrown by catapults. We also hear of barbed grappling irons and shields piled with red-hot sand that were then dropped on the besiegers who could have had no defence against such an attack.[236] One can only imagine the total devastation in the city that must have been caused by the constant need for building material for new defensive works as well as repair work on the walls

I have suggested earlier that Alexander tended to attempt to use land based tactics at sea, due to his complete lack of any naval warfare experience. We see Alexander's inability or unwillingness to modify his naval tactics clearly in his reactive measures towards the end of the siege. In order for the Phoenician navy to properly engage the fortifications the water had to be cleared of rocks, apparently thrown into the sea to prevent enemy ships getting too close to the walls. Alexander set his ships to clearing the area, but the Tyrians reacted by equipping a number of ships in such a way that if they sailed close to the anchored Phoenician vessels they would cut the mooring ropes; the Phoenician ships had to be anchored as they tried to winch the blocks on board, also using ropes. Alexander's first response is telling; he set up a defensive screen of ships to protect those that were vulnerable. This is exactly the tactic that he used to protect the workers on the mole, essentially to construct a solid barrier. It was only after the Tyrians used divers to cut the ropes that Alexander started using chains.[237] In this incident, as with earlier ones on the mole, we see Alexander in a reactive posture, something we do not normally expect.

The defenders' final gambit was to risk a naval sortie. They had noticed that the Cypriot fleet, which was guarding the northern harbour, withdrew every day at midday to eat their meal ashore. The Tyrians then manned three quinquiremes, three quadriremes and seven triremes with hand-picked men.[238] The Tyrians waited patiently until noon before beginning the sortie. The Tyrian vessels sailed from the Sidonian harbour and engaged the Cypriot fleet. What they encountered were ships that were either empty or had mere skeleton crews. Three Cypriot ships were sunk immediately and many others were driven onto the beach and disabled. One of the ships that was sunk was the flagship of King Pnytagoras of Cyprus. By pure chance, Alexander had not taken his usual afternoon nap, but had returned to the Phoenician fleet almost immediately after going ashore. We need not assume that this was any more than chance, such as some kind of advance intelligence; if it had been then the Cypriot fleet would surely not have been left so vulnerable. Upon hearing of the sortie, he ordered the Egyptian harbour to be sealed lest another attack be launched from there, and sailed with the remainder of the Phoenician fleet to the relief of the Cypriots. Most of the attacking Tyrian vessels were either captured or sunk as they failed to make the safety of the harbour before being engaged by Alexander, although the loss of life was small as the sailors simply swam to the relative safety of the island.[239]

With the mole at the very walls of Tyre, and all hope of protection from their fleet gone, the defenders were in an impossibly-desperate situation. The walls on the landward side of the city were, apparently, far too strong to be breached by the siege engines positioned there.[240] The walls to the north of the city proved to be equally strong, but the walls to the south were weaker. A considerable length of wall shook after a prolonged assault and finally collapsed. The breach in the wall was probably not large, and almost certainly not down to the foundations; more than likely a section of the ramparts gave way.[241] This was still key, however, as it meant the attackers did not have to fear red-hot sand or any other defensive countermeasures as they made their final assault. Arrian presents a picture of Alexander probing the city at all points, the defenders being 'caught in a ring of fire'.[242]

This was partly to try and force an entry and partly to draw defenders away from the section he wished to concentrate upon. The Tyrian resistance was at the same time impressive and desperate; they threw back the Macedonians at the breach and resisted Alexander's attempt to force both the Sidonian and Egyptian harbours.

After the repulse at the breach there was a lull in the fighting. Alexander may have offered terms to the Tyrians. If the offer was real, it was not popular amongst the Macedonian high command; only Amyntas, son of Adromenes, supported it.[243] The Tyrians were given two days to surrender, but on the third day the final assault began and their fate was sealed. The attack began with an artillery barrage that is highly reminiscent of World War II offensives, and was a fundamental ingredient of *Blitzkrieg*. After the naval barrage, a small unit of hypaspists, under Admetus, assaulted the breach. Admetus was killed by a spear before gaining the walls, but Alexander, who was also present, pressed forward and soon the southern sector of the city walls was in Macedonian hands. It is clear that the troops were well drilled and well commanded; they did not simply pour into the city as may have been expected, but remained in the vicinity of the walls to ensure the breach was held as more troops were brought forward.[244]

The breach was followed by panic and a general collapse of the Tyrian defences. The Phoenician fleet successfully forced an entry into the Egyptian harbour and made short work of the remainder of the enemy fleet stationed there. The Cypriot fleet had similar success to the north. Most of the Tyrian soldiers that remained alive withdrew to the shrine of Agenor, the father of Cadmus who was the legendary founder of Tyre and Sidon, with the intention of making a last stand; they were not disappointed. The slaughter was terrible; the Macedonians were allowed to vent their fury at such a brutal siege upon those that had survived. Some 8,000 Tyrians were killed and the remaining 30,000 were sold into slavery, as was the usual practice.[245]

The capture of Tyre is usually regarded as one of Alexander's finest achievements in the field of warfare. This is not without some justification: Tyre was a seemingly impregnable island fortress that was heavily defended and commanded by an extremely talented king, Azemilcus. Upon closer examination of the events of the siege, however, we see that many of Alexander's great innovations were in fact enforced reactions to the ingenuity of the Tyrians. We also see Alexander making a number of key errors, such as not defending the mole, or its workers, and not anticipating a noon sortie against his fleet. We see Alexander's lack of creativity as an admiral, using essentially land-based tactics for his fleet. Having said this, however, Alexander clearly shows himself to be eminently capable of adapting to new situations and new defensive measures with increasingly elaborate ideas of his own. We should also note that King Azemilcus of Tyre was one of the most able commanders Alexander ever faced, and should be given the due honour and recognition that he deserves.

Alexander's real genius was two-fold: firstly, the capacity to modify a relatively small parcel of strategies and tactics to meet the needs of every situation, every enemy and every type of terrain that he encountered; secondly, it was his ability to truly inspire men to ever greater achievements: his men showed repeatedly that they would do almost anything for their king and only finally said 'no more' when they had reached the very ends of the earth in India.

The life of Alexander is a remarkable nexus of events that is virtually unparalleled in history. Alexander was, perhaps, the finest military mind the world had yet seen: coupled with this was his inheritance from his father of one of the greatest armies of the ancient world. Had Alexander been born in less auspicious circumstances, we can only imagine how very different history would have been. These two factors – genius and circumstance – combined to enable the Macedonians to create, in less than a decade, an empire that spanned the known world. Alexander's achievements are legendary and worthy of study: rightly so.

Notes and References

—∭—

1 Clausewitz, 5.111.
2 Thucydides, 5.71.1; *cf.* Xenophon, *Hellenica*, 4.2.18-19.
3 *FGrH*, 72 F 4. Anaximenes was an historian of the mid-4th century who wrote a work on Philip of Macedon called the *Philippica*. There is a tradition, although untrustworthy, that he was an early tutor of Alexander. Anaximenes' work survives only in fragments, but it is clear, even from these, that he is less critical of either Philip or Alexander than was Theopompus: *FGrH*, 115 F 348. Theopompus was a contemporary of Anaximenes and his work bears the same title. His work, again fragmentary, appears to be very hostile to Philip.
4 Thucydides, 2.100.2.
5 Polyaenus, 2.1.17, (on 394 BC); Xenophon, *HG*, 5.2.40, (on 379 BC).
6 Demosthenes, *Second Olynthiac*, 2.19; this rather disparaging reference could refer to either a select body or all of the heavy infantry.
7 Diodorus, 17.17.3.
8 Polyaenus, 4.2.10.
9 Frontinus, 2.1.9; Diodorus, 16.85.5-87; Polyaenus, *Strat.* 4.2.2; Plutarch, *Alex*, 9.3; Diodorus, 17.2.3; Arrian, 7.6; Plutarch, *Alex*, 71.
10 Curtius, 3.2.13-14.
11 Lloyd, 1996, 172 on corporate unity.
12 Plutarch, *Alex*, 40.
13 Plutarch, *Alex*, 15.
14 Plutarch, *Alex*, 73.
15 Curtius, 4.16.31-3.
16 Diodorus, 17.17.4; 17.17.5.
17 Arrian, 3.11.9; Curtius, 4.13.28; Diodorus, 17.57.3.
18 Arrian, 5.12 *ff*.
19 Arrian, 3.16.11; 4.24.10; 4.22.7.
20 Arrian, 4.17.1.
21 Arrian, 4.22.1.
22 Arrian, 4.24.1; 4.25.6; 4.28.8.
23 Arrian, 4.22.7.
24 Arrian, 4.22.7.
25 Arrian, 6.6.1.
26 Appian, 11.19.7-10; Koechly, 3.223-4; Aelian, *Tact*, B. 533.
27 Theophrastus, *Hist Pl.*, 3.12.3; Asclepiodotus, *Tact*, 5.1; Polybius, 18.29; 29.2; Aelian, *Tact*, 14.
28 Aelian, *Tact*, 11; Polybius, 12.19.7.
29 Arrian, 1.1.9; 3.13.5-6.
30 Arrian, 1.4.1-3; 1.6.1-4.

31 Xenophon, *Cyropaedia*, 7.178; Diodorus, 17.57.5; Aelian, *Tact*, 11.4-5.
32 Curtius, 3.3.26-7
33 Polyaenus, *Strat*, 4.2.10.
34 Asclepiodotus, *Tact*, 5.
35 Arrian, 2.23.2; 4.23.6; 6.6.1; 7.21.3; 7.11.3. Every modern editor, with the exception of the Loeb translation by Brunt, has emended the text to read *pezhetairoi* in every case.
36 Arrian, 2.23.2.
37 Diodorus, 7.5.40; Plutarch, *Alexander*, 51.6; Curtius, 6.8.24; Curtius, 7.5.40.
38 For example, Arrian, 4.21.9; 4.30.3 and Curtius 5.2.3.*ff.*
39 Arrian, 4.30.6.
40 Arrian, 1.22.7.
41 Arrian, 3.16.10; Curtius 5.1.40.
42 Arrian, 4.24.10.
43 Diodorus, 19.28.1.
44 Diodorus, 17.65.2*ff.*
45 Diodorus, 17.17.4.
46 Bosworth, 1980, 98.
47 Contra; Bosworth, 1980, 99; 'we can no longer dogmatically assume that Ptolemy's figures are correct', but does not offer a positive answer, only that the discrepancies 'cannot be explained in the present state of the evidence'.
48 Diodorus, 17.17.4.
49 Diodorus, 17.17.4.
50 Polybius, 9.19.2.
51 Arrian, 3.16.10; Curtius, 5.1.40; Diodorus, 17.65.1.
52 Arrian, 4.6.2; 3.7.
53 Arrian, 1.14.6; 2.9.2; 3.12.3.
54 Diodorus, 17.17.4.
55 Arrian, 1.12.7; 1.14.1, 1.14.6; 2.9.2; 3.12.3; 3.18.2; 3.20.1; 3.21.2.
56 Plutarch *Alexander* 16.3; see also Hamilton, 1969, 40.
57 Arrian, 1.12.7; 14.1; 2.9.3; 3.11.8. etc.
58 Arrian, 1.2.5; 12.7; 11.9.3; 2.9.3.
59 Arrian, 4.23.1; 4.22.7; 4.22.1 (Craterus); Arrian 4.17.3 (Coenus).
60 Arrian, 1.24.3; 3.29.7; 4.4.6-7; Diodorus, 17.57.1.
61 Arrian, 1.24.3.
62 Arrian, 1.18.3; 2.20.4.
63 Arrian, 3.29.7.
64 Arrian, 6.6.1.
65 Arrian, 6.6.1; 6.7.2; 6.9.1.
66 Arrian, 6.11.8; 6.13.1.
67 Brunt, 1963, 30.
68 Hammond, 1998, 418; Hammond, 1980, 455*ff*; Hammond, 1980, 191*f.*
69 Arrian, 2.7.3; 10.2; 16.8; 3.9.3.
70 Brunt, 1963, 31.
71 Arrian, 5.11.3; 5 12.2; 5.2.2-4; 3.6; 6.2.3.
72 Arrian, 3.24.1.
73 Arrian, 5.12.2; 16.4; *cf.* Curtius 9.2.24.
74 Arrian, 7.6.3.

75 Arrian, 6.27.3.
76 Arrian, 7.6.3.
77 Fredricksmeyer, 2000, 137*ff.*
78 Arrian, 5.12.2; 6.7.2.
79 Koechly, 3.215.6; 3.223-24.
80 Asclepiodotus, *Tact.* 1.3.
81 Appian, 11.19.7-10; Arrian, 7.6.5; Aelian, *Tact.*12; Strabo, 10.1.12.
82 Arrian, 1.15.6; Polybius, 6.25.6;11.8.4.
83 Markle, 1977, 333, believes there to have been no significant difference in any way between the sarissa used by the cavalry and that used by the infantry, further believing that there was no difference in size or weight between the spear point at each end of the shaft of the cavalry sarissa.
84 Andronicos, 1970, 91-107.
85 Strabo, 10.1.12.
86 Arrian, 3.11.10.
87 Bosworth, 1988, 264.
88 Diodorus, 17.74.3.
89 Diodorus, 17.74.4; 17.57.2.
90 Curtius, 3.2.10*ff.*
91 Diodorus, 17.17.3*f.*
92 Thucydides, 6.43.
93 Diodorus, 15.44.2-4.
94 Diodorus, 15.44.2-4; Nepos, *Iphicrates* 9.1.3-4; Best, 1969, 102 (quote).
95 Parke, 1933, 21.
96 Polyaenus, 4.2.8; *cf.* Diodorus, 16.35.3.
97 Demosthenes, 3.49.
98 For example at Corinth (Polybius, 38.3.3), Sicyon (Demosthenes, 17.16), and in Ambracia (Diodorus, 17.3.3).
99 Diodorus, 17.17.3.
100 The table is an adaptation of that in Griffith, 1935, 20-1.
101 Diodorus, 17.17.3.
102 Arrian, 1.18.3.
103 Arrian, 3.5.3; the two Egyptians were Doloaspis and Petisis. Each was to have control over half of the country, but Petisis refused the appointment (the reason is not known) and so Doloaspis was given the whole province.
104 Curtius, 4.8.4.
105 Bosworth, 1980, 276.
106 Arrian, 2.9.3.
107 Fraser, 1996, 240-43; gives all of the possible foundations.
108 Diodorus, 17.49.5; Curtius, 10.2.8.
109 Arrian, 1.17.8; 1.24.3; 2.5.1; 3.18.1.
110 Curtius, 4.10.16.
111 Diodorus, 17.106.2*f.*
112 Diodorus, 17.106.3.
113 Badian, 1961.
114 Arrian, 7.23.1; 7.24.3-4; that is to say after the decree had been enacted.
115 Arrian, 1.18.7.
116 Arrian, 1.18.8.

117　Arrian, 1.18.7.
118　Arrian, 1.20.1; the following section relies heavily on Bosworth, 1980, 141*ff.*
119　Diodorus, 17.22.5.
120　Curtius, 3.1.19-20.
121　Arrian, 2.2.3.
122　Diodorus, 17.22.5.
123　Arrian, 2.2.4.
124　Arrian, 2.2.3; Curtius, 3.1.19-20.
125　Arrian, 3.2.3-7; Curtius, 3.1.19.
126　Arrian, 3.2.6.
127　Hauben, 1972, 56.
128　Arrian, 2.19.6; 2.20.1.
129　Arrian, 2.20.1.
130　Curtius, 4.3.11; Plutarch, *Alexander.* 24.5.
131　Diodorus, 14.41.6.
132　Diodorus, 14.41.4-42.1.
133　Thucydides, 2.75-8 (Plataea); Thucydides 3.20-3 (Syracuse).
134　Aristophanes, *The Birds*, 363. Dunbar, 1998, does not even consider that the 'machines' in question may have been catapults.
135　Diodorus, 13.54.7*ff*; Diodorus, 13.59.8*ff.*
136　Chronicles, 2.26.15.
137　Ezekiel, 4.2; 21.22.
138　Pliny, *Natural History* 7.201.
139　Sun Tzu (Tr. Cleary), 68; 71; 72. Sun Tzu was a Chinese military philosopher, c.500; he was an advocate of the bloodless victory, and of never fighting a battle unless victory was certain.
140　Diodorus, 16.74.4; 75.3; Arrian 1.22.2
141　Marsden, 1969, 58.
142　Thucydides, 2.76; Thucydides 3.22.
143　Plutarch, *Mor.* 191E.
144　Diodorus, 14.43.3.
145　Heron, 81.5-7.
146　Marsden, 1969, 17.
147　Curtius, 4.6.9.
148　Polyaenus, 2.38.
149　Arrian, 1.6. *cf.* Fuller, 1958, 226; claimed this to be 'the first recorded use of catapults as field artillery', although he is mistaken, since the Onomarchus incident occurred some years before.
150　Arrian, 4.4.
151　Curtius, 7.6.8.
152　Arrian, 7.23.
153　Bosworth, 1988, 273.
154　Arrian, 1.28.4.
155　Arrian, 4.13.4.
156　Arrian, 4.22 (Gorgias, Cleitus, Meleager); 4.24 (Coenus, Attalus); 4.25 (Polyperchon); 4.27 (Alcestas).
157　Curtius, 5.2.3.

158 Arrian, 3.16.11; *cf.* Curtius, 5.2.6; Diodorus, 17.65.2-4.
159 Arrian, 3.18.5.
160 Arrian, 3.27.
161 Arrian, 3.17, 4.3, 4.30.
162 Diodorus, 17.61.
163 Arrian, 2.12.
164 Arrian, 1.22.
165 Arrian, 4.16.
166 Arrian, 6.6 as *taxiarch*; 6.28, as bodyguard.
167 Arrian, 4.22; 5.12.
168 Justin 11.6.4.
169 Arrian, 1.1.4-1.9.8; The Illyrian campaign to the fall of Thebes; Strabo, 7.3.8*ff*;
    Diodorus, 17.8.1*ff*.
170 Arrian, 1.1.4; Diodorus, 17.3.5; Ashley, 1998, 166.
171 Arrian, 1.1.5.
172 Arrian, 1.1.7.
173 Arrian, 1.1.7-9; *cf.* Bloedow, 1996, 121.
174 Arrian, 1.1.7-9.
175 Arrian, 1.2.1; 1.2.2.
176 Arrian, 1.2.2.
177 Devine, 1988, 3; calls this device a 'pawn sacrifice', but incorrectly claims that it was
    first employed at the Granicus in 334.
178 Arrian, 3.29.4.
179 Xenophon, *Anabasis*, 1.5.10.
180 Arrian, 1.4.2.
181 Arrian, 1.5.5; 1.5.8.
182 Arrian, 1.6.1; Devine, 1983, 213; *cf* Hammond, 1974, 82.
183 Arrian, 1.6.2.
184 Arrian, 3.9.6
185 Curtius, 3.7.5-7; Arrian, 2.6.1.
186 Arrian, 2.5.6.
187 Curtius, 3.2.1-9.
188 Arrian, 2.6.3-7; Plutarch, *Alexander*, 20.1-2; Diodorus, 17.32.3.
189 Curtius, 3.3.1.
190 Diodorus, 17.32.4; Curtius, 38.24.
191 Plutarch, *Alexander*, 20.3.
192 Plutarch, *Alexander*, 20.4.
193 Arrian, 2.7.1*f.*
194 Arrian, 2.7.2.
195 Arrian, 2.6.2.
196 Polybius, 12.17.4-5; citing Callisthenes.
197 Arrian, 2.7.3-9.
198 Polybius, 12.19.5-6; *cf.* Arrian, 11.8.2; Curtius, 3.9.12.
199 Devine, 1985b, 49
200 Arrian, 2.8.6; Curtius, 3.9.2; Polybius, 12.18.2.
201 Arrian, 2.8.6; *cf* Polybius, 12.17.7.
202 Curtius, 3.9.5.

203 Arrian, 2.8.8; Plutarch, *Alexander*, 18.6.
204 Diodorus, 17.31.2; Justin, 9.9.1; Curtius, 3.2.4-9.
205 Curtius, 3.8.27*f*.
206 Curtius, 3.8.27-28; *cf* Arrian, 2.8.5.
207 Arrian, 2.9.2.
208 Arrian 2.8.9.
209 Curtius, 3.11.15; Arrian, 2.11.4.
210 Curtius, 3.2.6, 9-5.
211 Arrian, 2.11.2-3.
212 Curtius, 3.11.1; *cf* Diodorus, 33.2-3; Devine, 1985b, 51.
213 Curtius, 3.11.1.
214 Curtius, 3.11.2-4.
215 Arrian, 2.10.3; 2.10.5.
216 Arrian, 2.10.4; 2.11.4; Curtius, 3.11.7-8; 3.11.11; Diodorus, 17.33.5; 17.34.2-7; Arrian, 2.11.4.
217 Curtius, 4.2.2.
218 Arrian, 2.15.7.
219 Curtius, 4.2.4.
220 Arrian, 2.16.6; Curtius, 4.2.5 (quote).
221 Curtius, 4.2.6-15; Diodorus, 17.40.2*ff*; Atkinson, 1980, 295.
222 Arrian, 2.18.3, Curtius, 4.2.9; Curtius, 4.2.11.
223 Pliny, *NH*, 7.56.209; *cf* Thucydides, 13.50.5; Polyaenus, 1.22.4*ff*; Curtius, 4.3.26.
224 Arrian, 2.17.1; Curtius ,4.2.17*f*.
225 Diodorus, 14.48.3,51; *cf* Bosworth, 1980, 240.
226 Arrian, 2.18.3.
227 Arrian, 2.19.1*ff*.
228 Arrian, 2.19.6; Bosworth, 1980, 241 (quote).
229 Arrian, 2.20.1-3.
230 Arrian, 2.20.4.
231 Curtius, 4.3.13; Arrian, 2.20.6
232 Diodorus, 45.2.
233 Arrian, 2.21.7; Diodorus, 45.2.
234 Marsden, 1969, 101;103.
235 Arrian, 2.21.2; Diodorus, 45.5-6; 46.2.
236 Arrian, 2.21.3; Diodorus, 43.1-2; Curtius, 4.3.24-5.
237 Arrian, 2.21.4.
238 Arrian, 2.21.8.
239 Arrian, 2.22.1*f*.
240 Arrian, 2.22.6-7; Curtius, 4.3.13-18; Diodorus, 43.3-44.5.
241 Diodorus, 43.4, states that the wall was thrown down to the length of a *plethron*; Arrian, 2.22.7.
242 Arrian, 2.22.7.
243 Diodorus, 17.45.7.
244 Arrian, 2.24.3; Bosworth, 1980, 253.
245 Arrian, 2.24.4; Curtius, 4.2.15; Arrian, 2.24.4; Arrian, 2.24.5; Diodorus, 17.46.4, gives the number of captives at 13,000 and claims 2,000 were crucified. Curtius, 4.4.15, adds 15,000 who were smuggled out to Sidon: highly unlikely, but these figures also total 30,000.

Bibliography

—⟋ꞁꞁ⟍—

Anderson, J K, *Military Theory and Practice in the Age of Xenophon* (Berkley, 1970)

Anspach, A E, *De Alexandri Magni expeditione Indica* (Leipzig, 1903).

Ashley, J R, *The Macedonian Empire: The Era of Warfare Under Philip II and Alexander the Great* (London, 1998)

Atkinson, J C, *A Commentary on Q. Curtius Rufus' Historiae Alexandri Magni Books 3 and 4* (Amsterdam, 1980)

Badian, E, 'The Battle of the Granicus: A New Look', *Ancient Macedonia 2* (Thessalokini, 1977), 271-293

Badian, E, 'Alexander at Peucelaotis', *CQ* 37, 1987, 117-28.

Badian, E, 'Agis III. Revisions and Reflections', in I. Worthington (ed.), *Ventures into Greek History* (Oxford, 1994), 258-92

Bauer, A, 'Die Schlacht bei Issos', *Ost. Jb* 2, 1899, 105-128

Beloch, K J, *Griechische Geschichte* (Berlin, 1923)

Berve, H, *Das Alexanderreich auf prosopographischer Grundlage* (Munich, 1926)

Bigwood, J M, 'Ctesias as Historian', *Phoenix* 32, 1978, 19-41

Bloedow, E F, 'On 'Wagons' and 'Shields': Alexander's Crossing of Mt. Haemus in 335 BC', *The Ancient History Bulletin* 10.3-4, 1996, 119-130

Bose, P, *Alexander the Greats Art of Strategy* (London, 2003)

Bosworth, A B, 'Philip II and Upper Macedonia', *CQ* 21, 1971, 93-105

Bosworth, A B, 'Arrian and the Alexander Vulgate', *Foundation Hardt Entretiens* 22 (Geneva, 1976), 1-46

Bosworth, A B, *Commentary on Arrian's History of Alexander: Vol I* (Oxford, 1980)

Bosworth, A B, 'Alexander and the Iranians', *JHS* 100, 1980b, 1-21

Bosworth, A B, *Conquest and Empire, The Reign of Alexander the Great* (Cambridge, 1988)

Bosworth, A B, *Commentary on Arrian's History of Alexander: Vol II* (Oxford, 1995)

Bosworth, A B & Baynham, E J (eds.), *Alexander the Great in Fact and Fiction* (Oxford, 2000)

Brunt, P A, 'Persian Accounts of Alexander's Campaigns', *CQ* 12, 1962, 141-55

Brunt, P A, 'Alexander's Macedonian Cavalry', *JHS* 83, 1963, 27-46

Brunt, P A, *Arrian: History of Alexander and Indica* (Loeb Classical Library) I-II (Cambridge, 1976-83)

Burn, A R, *Alexander the Great and the Hellenistic World* (London, 1947)

Burn, A R, 'Notes on Alexander's Campaigns, 332-330', *JHS* 72, 1952, 81-91

Casson, L, *Ships and Seamen in the Ancient World* (Princeton, 1971)

Cook, J M, *The Persian Empire* (New York, 1983)

Davis, E W, 'The Persian Battle Plan at the Granicus', *James Sprunt Studies in History and Political Science* 46, 1964, 34-44

Delbruck, H, *Geschichte der Kriegskunst im Rahmen der Politischen Geschichte* (Berlin, 1920); available in English, translated by W J Renfroe, *History of the Art of War within the Framework of Political History* (reprinted London, 1975).

Devine, A M, 'The Location of the Battlefield of Issus', *LCM* 5, 1980, 3-10

Devine, A M, A Note on Tactical Terms', *LCM* 7, 1982, 62-63

Devine, A M, 'Embolon: A Study in Tactical Terminology', *Phoenix* 37, 1983, 201-217

Devine, A M, 'The Strategies of Alexander the Great and Darius III in the Issus Campaign', *Ancient World* 12, 1985a, 25-38

Devine, A M, 'Grand Tactics at the Battle of Issus', *Ancient World* 12, 1985b, 39-59

Devine, A M, 'The Battle of Gaugamela', *Ancient World* 13, 1986, 87-116

Devine, A M, 'The Battle of the Hydaspes: A Tactical and Source-Critical Study', *Ancient World* 16, 1987, 91-113

Devine, A M, 'A Pawn-Sacrifice at the Battle of the Granicus', *Ancient World* 18, 1988, 3-20

Dinsmoor, W B, *Archons of Athens* (Cambridge, Mass, 1931)

Dittberner, W, *Issos, ein Beitrag zur Geschichte Alexanders des Großen* (Berlin, 1908)

Dodge, T A, *Alexander the Great Vols I-II* (Boston, 1890)

von Domaszewski, A, 'Die Phalangen Alexanders und Caesars Legionen', *Heidelberger Sitz. – Ber. Phil. – hist. Kl.* 16, 1925, 50-65.

Doherty, P, *Alexander the Great: The Death of a God* (London, 2004)

Dunbar, N, *Birds: with Introduction and Commentary* (Oxford, 1998)

Eadie, J W, 'The Development of Roman Mailed Cavalry', *JRS* 57, 1967, 161-173

Eggermont, P H L, 'Alexander's Campaign in Gandhara and Ptolemy's list of Indo-Scythian Towns', *Orientalia Lovaniensia Periodica* 1, 1970, 63-123

Eggermont, P H L, 'Ptolemy the Geographer and the People of the Dards', *OLP* 15, 1984, 191-200.

Ellis, J R, 'Alexander's Hypaspists Again', *Historia* 24, 1975, 617-618

Engels, D W, *Alexander the Great and the Logistics of the Macedonian Army* (California, 1978)

English, S 'Hoplites or Peltasts: The Macedonian 'Heavy' Infantry', *Ancient Warfare* 2.1, 2008, 32-35

Errington, R M, 'Bias in Ptolemy's History of Alexander', *CQ* 19 (1969), 233-242

Errington, R M, *A History of Macedonia* (California, 1990)

Foss, C, 'The Battle of the Granicus River: A New Look', *Ancient Macedonia 2* (Thessalokini, 1977), 495-502

Fraser, P M, *Cities of Alexander the Great* (Oxford, 1996)

Fuller, J F C, *The Generalship of Alexander the Great* (London, 1958)

Green, P, *Alexander of Macedon, 356-323 B.C.* (Oxford, 1974)

Griffith, G T, *The Mercenaries of the Hellenistic World* (Cambridge, 1935)

Griffith, G T, 'Alexander's Generalship at Gaugamela', *JHS* 67, 1947, 77-89

Griffith, G T, 'A Note on the Hipparchies of Alexander', *JHS* 83, 1963, 68-75

Griffith, G T, 'Peltasts and the Origins of the Macedonian Phalanx', in H J Dell (ed.), *Ancient Macedonian Studies in Honour of Charles F. Edson* (Thessalonika, 1981)

Guderian, H, *Achtung-Panzer!* (Munich, 1937): available in English, translated by C. Duffy *Achtung-Panzer!* (London, 1995)

Hackett, J (ed.), *Warfare in the Ancient World* (London, 1989)

Hamilton, J R, 'Three Passages in Arrian', *CQ* 5, 1955, 217-21

Hamilton, J R, 'The Cavalry Battle at the Hydaspes', *JHS* 76, 1956, 26-31

Hamilton, J R, 'The Letters in Plutarch's *Alexander*', *PACA* 4, 1961, 9-20

Hamilton, J R, *Plutarch, Alexander: A Commentary* (London, 1969)

Hamilton, J R, *Alexander the Great* (London, 1973)

Hammond, N G L, 'Alexander's Campaign in Illyria', *JHS* 94, 1974, 66-87

Hammond, N G L and Griffith, G T, *A History of Macedonia ii: 550-336 BC* (Oxford, 1979)

Hammond, N G L, 'The Battle of the Granicus River', *JHS* 100, 1980, 73-89

Hammond, N G L, *Alexander the Great: King Commander and Statesman* (London, 1980b)

Hammond, N G L, 'Some Passages in Arrian Concerning Alexander', *CQ* 30, 1980c, 455-76

Hammond, N G L, *Three Historians of Alexander the Great* (Cambridge, 1983)

Hammond, N G L and Walbank, F W, *History of Macedonia, vol. 3* (Oxford, 1988)

Hammond, N G L, *Alexander the Great: King, Commander and Statesman* (Bristol, 1989)

Hammond, N G L, *The Macedonian State. The Origins, Institutions and History* (Oxford, 1989b)

Hammond, N G L, 'The Macedonian Navies of Philip and Alexander Until 330 B.C.', *Antichthon* 26, 1992, 30-41

Hammond, N G L, 'Some Passages in Polyaenus' Stratagems Concerning Alexander', *GRBS* 37, 1996, 23-54

Hammond, N G L, 'A Papyrus Commentary on Alexander's Balkan Campaign', *GRBS* 28, 1997, 332-348

Hammond, N G L, *The Genius of Alexander the Great* (London, 1997)

Hammond, N G L, 'Cavalry Recruited in Macedonia Down to 322 B.C.', *Historia* 47, 1998, 404-425

Hanson, V D, *The Western Way of War: Infantry Battle in Classical Greece*, (New York, 1989)

Harl, K W, 'Alexander's Cavalry Battle at the Granicus', *Polis and Polemos*, (Claremont, 1997), 303-326

Hasluck, F W, *Cyzicus* (Cambridge, 1910)

Hauben, H, 'The Command Structure of Alexander's Mediterranean Fleets', *Ancient Society* 3, 1972, 56

Heckel, W, *The Marshals of Alexander's Empire* (London, 1992)

Heckel, W, *The Wars of Alexander the Great: 336-323 BC* (Oxford, 2002)

Heckel, W, de Souza, P, and Llewellyn-Jones, L, *The Greeks at War: From Athens to Alexander* (Oxford, 2004)

Heckel, W, *The Conquests of Alexander the Great* (Cambridge, 2008)

Holt, F L, 'Alexander's Settlements in Central Asia', *Ancient Macedonia* 4, 1986, 315-323

Holt, F L, *Alexander the Great and Bactria* (Leiden, The Netherlands, 1989)

Holt, F L, *Into the Land of Bones: Alexander the Great in Afghanistan* (London, 2005)

Janke, A, *Auf Alexanders des Grossen Pfaden. Eine Reise durch Kleinasein* (Berlin, 1904)

Janke, A, 'Die Schlacht bei Issus', *Klio* 10, 1910, 137-177

Judeich, W, 'Die Schlacht am Granikos', *Klio*8, 1908, 372-97

Judeich, W, in Kromayer, J and Veith, G (eds.), *Antike Schlachtfelder IV* (Berlin, 1929)

Kaerst, J, *Geschichte des Hellenismus* (Leipzig, 1927)

Keegan, J, *The Mask of Command* (New York, 1987)

Keipert, H, 'Das Schlachtfeld am Granikos', *Globus* 32, 1887, 263*ff*

Kedar, B Z, *The Horns of Hattin* (London, 1992)

Kern, P B, *Ancient Siege Warfare* (London, 1999)

Kornemann, E, *Die Alexandergeschichte des Konigs von Aegypten* (Berlin, 1935)

Landels, J G, 'Ship-Shape and *Sambuca*-Fashion', *JHS* 86, 1966, 69-77

Lane Fox, R, *Alexander the Great* (London, 1973)

Leaf, W, *Strabo on the Troad* (Cambridge, 1923)

Lloyd, A B (ed.), *Battle in Antiquity* (London, 1996)

Lonsdale, D J, *Alexander: Killer of Men* (London, 2004)

Lorimer, H L, 'The Hoplite Phalanx', *BSA* 42, 1947, 76-138

Manti, P A, 'The Cavalry Sarissa', *Ancient World* 8, 1983, 73-80

Manti, P A, 'The Sarissa of the Macedonian Infantry', *Ancient World* 23.2, 1992, 31-42

Manti, P A, 'The Macedonian Sarissa, again', *Ancient World* 25.1, 1994, 77-91

Markle, M M, 'The Macedonian Sarissa, Spear, and Related Armour', *AJA* 81, 1977, 323-339

Markle, M M, 'Use of the Macedonian Sarissa by Philip and Alexander', *AJA* 82, 1978, 483-497

Markle, M M, 'Macedonian Arms and Tactics under Alexander the Great', *Studies in The History of Art* Vol 10, (Washington, 1982) 86-111

Marsden, E W, *The Campaign of Gaugamela* (Liverpool, 1964)

Marsden, E W, *Greek and Roman Artillery: Historical Developments* (Oxford, 1969)

Marsden, E W, *Greek and Roman Artillery: Technical Treatises* (Oxford, 1971)

May, E C, Stadler, G P, and Votan, J F, *Ancient and Medieval Warfare* (Wayne, N.J. 1984)

McQueen, E I, 'Quintus Curtius Rufus', in *Latin Biography*; ed. T A Dorey (London, 1967) 17-43

Messenger, C, *The Art of Blitzkrieg* (London, 1976)

Milns, R D, 'Alexander's Macedonian Cavalry and Diodorus 17.17.4', *JHS* 86, 1966, 167-168

Milns, R D, 'Philip II and the Hypaspists', *Historia 16, 1967, 509-12*

Milns, R D, *Alexander the Great* (London, 1968)

Milns, R D, 'The Hypaspists of Alexander III: Some Problems', *Historia* 20, 1971, 186-195

Miltner, F, 'Alexander's Strategie bei Issos', *Ost Jh.* 28, 1933, 69-78

Mixter, J R, 'The Length of the Macedonian Sarissa During the Reigns of Philip II and Alexander the Great', *Ancient World* 23.2, 1992, 21-29

Morrison, J S, and Williams, R T, *Greek Oared Ships 900-322B.C.* (Cambridge, 1968)

Morrison, A, 'Combat Psychology, and Persepolis', *Antichthon* 35, 2001, 30-44

Mughal, M R, 'Excavations at Tulamba, West Pakistan', *Pakistan Archaeology* 4, 1967, 1-152.

Murison, J A, 'Darius III and the Battle of Issus', *Historia* 21, 1972, 399-423

Papazoglu, F, *The Central Balkan Tribes in Pre-Roman Times* (Amsterdam, 1978)

Pearson, L, *The Lost Histories of Alexander the Great* (New York, 1960)

Parke, H W, *Greek Mercenary Soldiers* (Oxford, 1933)

Rahe, P A, 'The Annihilation of the Sacred Band at Chaeronea', *AJA* 85, 1981, 84-87

Renfroe, W J, *History of the Art of War within the Framework of Political History* (London, 1975)

Rhodes P J, and Osborne, R, *Greek Historical Inscriptions, 404-323 BC* (Oxford, 2007)

Rhodes, P J, *A History of the Classical Greek World: 478-323 BC* (Oxford, 2006)

Roisman, J, 'Ptolemy and His Rivals in His History of Alexander', *CQ* 34, 1984, 373-385

Romane, P, 'Alexander's Siege of Tyre', *Ancient World* 16, 1987, 79-90.

Romane, P, 'Alexander's Siege of Gaza – 332 B.C.', *Ancient World* 18, 1988, 21-30.

Rubin, B, 'Die Entstehung der Kataphraktenreiterei im Lichte der Chorezmischen Ausgrabungen', *Historia* 4, 1955, 264-83

Rutz, W, 'Zur Erzahlungskunst des Q. Curtius Rufus', *Hermes* 93, 1965, 370-82

Sage, M M, *Warfare in Ancient Greece* (London, 1996)

Schachermeyr, F, *Alexander der Grosse* (Vienna, 1973)

Schwartz, E, (ed. Pauley), *Realencyclopadie der Classischen Altertumswissenschaft* (Stuttgart, 1893)

Sekunda, N, *The Army of Alexander the Great* (London, 1984)

Shrimpton, G, 'The Persian Cavalry at Marathon', *Phoenix* 34, 1980, 20-37

Sidnell, P, *Warhorse: Cavalry in Ancient Warfare* (London, 2006)

Smith, V, *The Early History of India* (Oxford, 1914)

Snodgrass, A M, *Arms and Armour of the Greeks* (Ithaca, N.Y. 1967)

de Souza, P, Heckel W, and Llewellyn-Jones, L, *The Greeks at War: From Athens to Alexander* (Oxford, 2004)

Spence, I G, *The Cavalry of Ancient Greece; A Social and Military History* (Oxford, 1993)

Stark, F, *Alexander's Path* (London, 1958)

Stein, A, 'The Site of Alexander's Passage of the Hydaspes and the Battle with Porus', *Geographical Journal* 80, 1932, 31-46

Stein, A, *Archaeological Reconnaissance's in North-Western India and South-Eastern Iran* (London, 1937)

Stein, A, 'Notes on Alexander's Crossing of the Tigris and the Battle of Arbela', *Geographical Journal* 100, 1942, 155-164.

Strasburger, H, *Ptolemaios und Alexander* (Leipzig, 1934)

Strasburger, H, 'Alexander's Zug Durch die Gedrosişche Wüste', *Hermes* 80, 1952, 456-493

Talbert, R J A (ed.), *Barrington Atlas of the Greek and Roman World* (Oxford, 2000)

Tarn, W W, *Alexander the Great: Vols. I-II* (Cambridge, 1948)

Tarn, W W, *The Greeks of Bactria and India*, 3rd ed. (Chicago, 1985)

Tod, M N, *A Selection of Greek Historical Inscriptions. 2: From 403 to 323 BC* (Oxford, 1948)

Tritle, L A, (ed.), *The Greek World in the Fourth Century* (London, 1997)

Veith, G, 'Der Kavalleriekampf in der Schlacht am Hydaspes', *Klio* 8, 1908, 131-53.

Wilcken, U, *Alexander the Great* (London, 1932)

Index

—⁓—